THE BOY WHO FAILED DODGEBALL

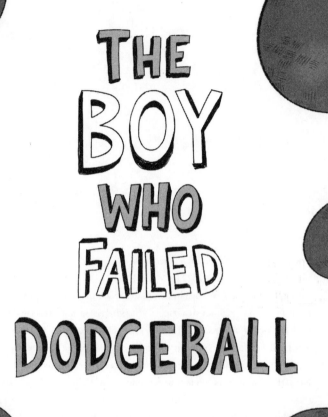

THE
BOY
WHO
FAILED
DODGEBALL

A MEMOIR BY JORDAN SONNENBLICK

Scholastic Press / New York

Library of Congress Cataloging-in-Publication Data available

ISBN 978-1-338-74960-1

10 9 8 7 6 5 4 3 2 1   22 23 24 25 26

Printed in Italy   183

First edition, April 2022

Book design by Christopher Stengel

To my fellow members of Class 1A at I.S. 61:
I hope life has treated you kindly, and that
you've managed to avoid moldy books
for the past 41 years.

And to everyone who's ever worn the red
blazer of the I.S. 61 Morning Band:
we truly were the best. Or at least,
one larger-than-life man
made us believe we were.

1. Blood and Fireworks

In my almost-twelve years on this planet, I'd like to think I've learned a few things. So I've decided to share my hard-earned wisdom with all you other young people out there. Let's start with the best piece of advice I can possibly give you: Don't be born on a major national holiday. Sure, it's great that you will never have to go to school on your birthday. But being born on the Fourth of July nearly killed me.

Multiple times.

It started before I was even born. My dad, who is a psychiatrist, got drafted to be an army doctor in the Vietnam War just after my parents found out my mom was pregnant. By the time I came around, my mom, my dad, and my big sister, Lissa, lived on a big military base in Missouri called Fort Leonard Wood. My mom went into labor late at night on July 3, 1969, so my dad called the hospital. There were only two doctors on the staff who delivered babies, and one was off base for the big July 4 weekend. The other was at the base's massive holiday fireworks party, super drunk.

Anyway, my dad and a couple of the other base doctors

found the drunk guy, threw him in the shower, and gave him a whole lot of coffee. When my mom was ready to give birth, he was mostly just incredibly hungover. My mom saw that he looked kind of sick and shaky, so she made a deal with him. She said that if he delivered me safe and sound, she would name me after him.

His name was Ted. Not Theodore, just Ted.

I guess he didn't drop me or anything, because my parents named me Jordan Ted Sonnenblick.

Then there was the biggest July 4 ever: the Bicentennial. On July 4, 1976, when I turned seven, the country went all in on the grandest birthday celebration in its history. In Staten Island, New York, where I have lived since I was thirteen months old, kids painted every fire hydrant red, white, and blue. (The older kids let me paint two white stripes on the one at the end of my block!) New York Harbor, from the Statue of Liberty all the way to the Verrazano-Narrows Bridge, was packed with hundreds of tall sailing ships, big fancy yachts, fireboats, barges, and small speedboats. There were even dozens of US Navy ships. It was like a gigantic, very wet traffic jam.

A couple of days before the big event, teams of workers started to hang the largest American flag ever made between the two towers of the bridge. My richest friend, Steven Vitale, had a house on a big hill looking over the harbor, so my sister and I went over there to play with Steven and his sister and watch the flag go up. The girls were playing Hula-Hoop at the bottom of Steven's long, steep driveway while Steven and I took turns trying to skateboard down from the street to the house. This was kind of challenging, because the driveway wasn't perfectly smooth. It had lots of sharp pieces of gravel sticking up from the cement. Steven went inside for a drink break, but I decided to make one more run.

Somehow, just after I reached top speed, I lost my balance, went flying over the front of the board, and landed facedown.

My forehead must have hit one of those sharp pebbles. I think I was knocked out for a second, but it didn't hurt or anything. I stood up and started walking toward the girls, who took one look at me and ran screaming into the house. I couldn't figure out what was wrong until I felt something warm and wet dripping into my right eye.

Steven's mom came out, took me inside, and washed out the new dent in my forehead. By the time she was done bandaging me up, I was feeling pretty dizzy, so she took me to Steven's room, led me to the bed, and told me to rest. But Steven's room had a huge picture window that faced the water, and after a while, practice fireworks started going off.

If you've never gotten banged on the head, cut up, and knocked out, then locked in a room with the rockets' red glare and bombs bursting in air outside, I don't recommend it as a pleasure activity.

Two days later, I was feeling mostly recovered, aside from

the intense itch that was coming from under the gauze pad just above my eyebrow. My whole family went to the roof of the building where my dad's office was. The building was only a block from the harbor, so we had the best view in town for the parade of ships and the fireworks display. Everybody got plates and filled them up with hamburgers and hot dogs. As we settled in to eat with all my dad's doctor friends and their kids, a question popped into my head that I just had to ask somebody.

For as long as I could remember, all the grown-ups in my family had told me that the July Fourth fireworks were for me. But there had never been a gazillion sailing ships, a two-hundred-foot-tall flag on a bridge, or a huge, official citywide fireworks display before. Had I done something special to deserve this? It was important to know, so I'd remember to do it again next year. I didn't know what *bicentennial* meant, and it was all pretty confusing. I turned to my dad's friend Dr. Accettola and asked, "Why is July Fourth such a big deal this year?"

"Because this year is the two hundredth," he replied.

"But I'm only seven!" I exclaimed.

That was when it hit me. The celebration wasn't in my honor at all. I took my plate behind a big brick chimney, sat with my back resting against the bricks, and cried.

All this time, I had thought I was famous. But really, I was just a little nobody.

Do yourself a favor. If you don't want a lifetime of danger

and heartbreak, be born on some random Tuesday in October. Or maybe March. March is nice.

Because here's the thing about being born on July 4. It teaches you to love fireworks. To wish for bigger and bigger fireworks. And to hope that one day, you'll be such a big deal that the big fireworks *are* for you.

2. Pick Your Heroes Carefully

I can't remember a time when I didn't love Evel Knievel, the greatest stuntman of all time. He isn't just the greatest stuntman. He's, like, the guy who invented the whole job of "stuntman." Before Evel Knievel, guys who crashed their motorcycles, broke multiple bones, and ended up in a coma were just considered unlucky. Evel Knievel turned the near-fatal motorcycle accident into an art form. By the time I was in kindergarten, practically every kid in my class wanted to be Evel Knievel. It looked like so much fun! He always wore a red-white-and-blue jumpsuit, and there were always thousands of cheering, screaming fans lined up to watch his stunts. Wherever Evel went, the fireworks really *were* for him.

I remember being at my Aunt Iris's house in New Jersey when I was five, gathered around with all my cousins to wait for Evel Knievel's famous rocket jump across Snake River Canyon in Idaho. It was so incredible! The jump distance was more than a quarter of a mile! I didn't know what a quarter of a mile was, but it sounded like a lot. Evel got lowered into his custom Skycycle rocket by crane, two assistants strapped him into his seat and put his helmet on, and then we all held our breath.

The Skycycle shot up the gigantic ramp at 350 miles an hour. We cheered as it flew upward into the air over the canyon. Then the disaster happened: The parachute that was supposed to slow the Skycycle down at the end opened too early. We all sat there in shock as the TV announcers said Evel and his Skycycle were going to land in the rushing rapids of the canyon!

It was almost a bummer when he survived with only a broken nose.

That was the thing about Evel Knievel. You could never tell which was cooler: his successes or his failures. I mean, in his very first major stunt, before I was even born, he was trying to jump a motorcycle over a ninety-foot-long box of rattlesnakes and land between two mountain lions. Making the jump would have been amazing enough. But he actually landed a bit short and broke through the far end of the box, freeing the rattlesnakes as the crowd fled in horror.

Angry rattlesnakes everywhere?

Legendary.

It might seem nutty to idolize a guy who holds the Guinness record for the most broken bones in a lifetime. But kids in my class show up every year with Evel Knievel lunch boxes. I don't think I have ever met a boy who didn't have at least one or two Evel Knievel action figures lying around his room. The smart kids leave it right there. The maniacs like me have

spent their entire childhoods trying to live up to the legend.

On my block, we are all in on the stuntman lifestyle. We spend hours putting together ramps. We have short ramps. We have long ramps. We have steep ramps and gradual ramps. We even have ramps that make you land on other ramps.

Don't try that one at home.

Have there been injuries? You *bet* there have been injuries! Riding on my original bicentennial-model

Schwinn bike that looked like an Evel Knievel tribute with its stars-and-stripes paint job, my friend Peter Friedman once flew over the handlebars right in front of my house and left a skid mark made of skin on the street. Dougie Kaner, who lived two doors down from me until he moved to a new house last year, once landed on his chin and needed to get stitches. Then there was the time I was timing myself racing down the street and flew over the handlebars, removing all the skin from my left shoulder. My mom, who saw the whole thing from our front window, was afraid to come out of the house and roll me over, because she was literally afraid my whole face would be gone.

For a while, our favorite bike game was chicken, which involves two guys riding their bikes at each other at top speed to see who swerves first. That lasted until the Great Head-On Collision of 1978, in which Dougie and I *both* flew over the handlebars and knocked heads in midair.

If flying over the handlebars becomes an Olympic sport, the training center will be my block.

Then there was last year's most popular pastime, Kill the Guy on the Green Machine. I am sure you've all seen a Green Machine. You know, the grass-colored plastic tricycle with the small back wheels, the gigantic front wheel, and the two levers you yank if you want to steer? Well, for a while on our block, we would borrow a Green Machine from Eric Warheit, the younger kid who lived between my house and Dougie's, and then the brutal spectacle would begin as five or six other guys tried to deliberately crash into it.

What I figured out before anybody else is that the guy on the Green Machine is actually safer than the guys on the bikes chasing him, because his back is protected by a hard plastic seat and his front is protected by the gigantic wheel. Honestly, the only way the Green Machine rider can lose is if one of the bicycle riders attacks from the side and somehow manages to get his bike's front wheel between the edge of the Green Machine's seat and the mounting for the steering levers. That's only maybe a foot of room. Much more often, anybody who crashes into the Green Machine flies over his bike's handlebars.

At one point, the flying-over-the-handlebars thing got so out of hand that Dougie's mom said, "You know, somebody should really invent some kind of a . . . I don't know . . . a helmet for kids to wear when they ride bikes." Dougie and I laughed about that one for days.

I crash into things on purpose so often that you might even think I am fearless. But I have a secret nobody knows:

I am secretly terrified almost all the time.

I am scared I will die from an asthma attack.

I am scared that my three remaining grandparents will get cancer and die like my Nana Adele did when I was in second grade.

Most of all, for years and years, I have spent every Monday and Wednesday night lying awake in bed, afraid that my mom will crash her car on the forty-minute drive home from her night classes at Rutgers University in New Jersey.

Some people might think I am weird because I spend so much of my time and energy inventing new ways of crashing into stuff when I'm so scared of everything. But that isn't the really weird part. The really weird part is that the only time I am not afraid of death is when I am doing things that are actually death-defying.

Being in danger is one of the few things that make me feel safe.

3. September

If you think about it, sixth grade is a really terrible idea. You spend your whole life watching the big kids head off to middle school, and you think they seem so cool and grown-up. They're laughing with their friends, bragging about trouble they've gotten into and out of, teasing each other about crushes—which all makes middle school sound a million times more exciting than elementary school. By the end of fifth grade, you can't *wait* for the fall, and your daring new life of adventure.

Then September actually arrives, and you realize that sixth grade is a terrifying downhill death ride on hostile, shifting terrain. All of a sudden, you are with kids from like four different elementary schools. Everybody who was the best at something in the spring is just another nobody now. Were you the fastest kid at P.S. 45? News flash: You might not even be in the top ten at I.S. 61. Did you think that being the smartest kid at P.S. 16 made you special? Just wait till you see what the kids from P.S. 31 know already. There's a junior chess master from 45, a girl from 16 who has been in three

TV commercials already, a concert piano champion from 31.

And that's just the sixth grade. The seventh and eighth graders are even more advanced. Talented. *Huge.*

But your classmates are only one of the challenges you face. Instead of having to figure out one teacher who's going to be with you the whole day, you have a gajillion different teachers, and they all have different personalities. Some might be friendly. Some might be mean. Some might be the type that starts out seeming mean but is really friendly once you get to know them. And it's a sure thing that some are going to seem nice at first but *turn out* to be mean.

And every teacher wants you to have different supplies. Each one has a different way of assigning seats. Some want you to raise your hand and ask before you cross the room to sharpen your pencil. Some bark, "Why are you wasting my time asking whether you can walk fifteen feet? Do I look like your *mom*?"

But if you snap back, "No, my mom is pretty," *you're* the one who gets in trouble.

Then there are the rules of the school: the official ones that tell you things like when you can go to your locker and what kind of dorky gym shorts you have to buy, and the real, semi-secret ones like, "Never, ever use the bathroom outside the gym on the Concourse. Ever. EVER."

I haven't even mentioned the incredibly dense crowds in the hallways, the swarming hive of the cafeteria, the utter chaos of dismissal, or the nonstop noise. The night before my first day at I.S. 61, it all hits me. For months, I thought I was ready for this, but I'm not.

I am picturing the beginning of middle school as an extremely rapid, terrifying, and uncontrolled ride straight into a wall.

As it turns out, I am not so far off.

4. Attack of the Praying-Mantis Boy

My mom has set up a carpool with Dougie Kaner's mom. It's me, Dougie, and his cousin Geoff Straniere. I kind of know Geoff from living two doors down from Dougie most of my life. Dougie is my friend because we both love riding bikes and playing baseball. When Geoff is at Dougie's, though, he takes things to a different level. All of a sudden, we are amateur stuntmen.

Evel Knievel–level amateur stuntmen.

My end of Waldron Avenue is at the bottom of a valley. Because of the steep hill at the top of our block, all the houses from mine down to the Wards' are something like twelve feet lower than the ones on the next street over. This means the houses on that street have high rock walls at the far edge of their backyards to stop the yards from collapsing into ours. When Geoff is over, we never walk on the sidewalk from house to house. Instead, we climb up onto the narrow stone ledge at the back of one yard and then inch our way from yard to yard, climbing over the fences that separate the yards as we go. Do you know how scary it is to climb a high chain-link fence when your landing spot is less than a foot wide and overlooks a small cliff?

I do. And I kind of love it.

Geoff is like that with everything. Bike riding becomes a demolition derby. Conversations become insult battles. Drinking soda becomes a two-liter chugging contest. He makes everything frantic and crazy and exciting.

Also, slightly terrifying.

On the first day of school, Dougie, Geoff, and I are giggling through the whole car ride. I am totally nervous. This school has way over a thousand kids—almost four hundred just in the sixth grade! I switched elementary schools in the middle of fourth grade, and now I am transferring to yet another school zone. All the kids my age from my first school, P.S. 35, are going to I.S. 27. All the kids from my second school, P.S. 54, are headed off to I.S. 72. But my mom wanted me to go to I.S. 61 because it is something called an "arts magnet school." Basically, 61 is the best school in Staten Island for band, chorus, and orchestra, and any kid from anywhere on the island can go there as long as that kid is good at music. My old friend Peter Friedman is in the seventh grade at 61, and even though he isn't in band, his mom says the program is incredible. I play the drums and am really into it, so my mom signed me up. The problem is that I only know two kids in my whole grade: Dougie and Geoff. And it's not like they can introduce me to their friends, because they both went to private school. We are all we have.

I am excited to be in a band for the first time in my life, but the idea of getting thrown in with four hundred kids who don't know me is making my heart pound. When we get out of the car, we can't even get to the front doors of the building because there are hundreds and hundreds of other kids milling around between the open school gate and the entrance. The gate and the doors are connected by a cement path that is maybe fifteen feet wide and a hundred feet long, and every square inch of it is invisible because there are so many people packed together.

Also, everybody is yelling—or at least it seems that way. People are shouting out the names of their friends, finding each other, and making little islands of P.S. 45 kids, P.S. 16 kids, and P.S. 31 kids. I don't need to shout to find the only people I know, because they are walking in with me. That's kind of a good thing, because I am so much shorter than everybody else that there's no way I'd be able to see my old friends even if I had any.

After a few very sweaty minutes of being face-to-elbow with many random strangers, I hear a loud buzzer noise coming from a speaker at the top of the school's flagpole. This must be the signal for the doors to open, because I immediately feel the crowd starting to push me toward the building. At some point, a space opens up in front of me, and I realize I am not lined up with the doorway. The crowd is going to push me into the brick wall about ten feet to the right.

Oh, great! I am about to become the first kid in history to

die by getting smushed into the side of his school. All that will be left of me is a reddish-brown smear at the point of impact, and maybe a scrap of fabric from my jean jacket. A few years from now, even the stain will start to fade. I hope my parents will convince the school district to put up a tasteful brass plaque in my memory.

Not that anyone will care, because I haven't even met anybody yet.

I grab Doug by the sleeve and start tugging him to the left as hard as I can. He looks up, and his eyes open super wide as he sees what's happening. He catches Geoff's wrist and starts to pull.

We nearly make it through the doors without injury. Geoff gets in okay. Dougie does, too. Just as I am about to step through, I feel a surge of pressure against my back that sends me shooting forward. I clear the doorway, but before my eyes can adjust from the bright daylight to the dimness inside, I smash my right shoulder against something incredibly hard. It's the metal edge of the *next* door, which is just a few feet after the first.

Apparently, middle schools have air locks, like really big, unfriendly spaceships.

The whole arm goes numb, but I just keep walking through the air lock and into the first-floor hallway. Not that I could stop if I wanted to. I'd be trampled in seconds. The herd moves me around a couple of turns and into a huge auditorium. The next thing I know, a gigantic man with a bushy red mustache is yelling, "Sixth graders, find a seat! Let's get started!" into a microphone onstage.

I try to look around for Doug and Geoff, but I can't see them anywhere. This is partly because I am the third-shortest person in the room, and partly because the scene is total chaos, with everybody trying to grab seats next to their friends. The big dude at the front is getting louder and louder as he waits for us to be seated. I am still twirling around in little circles in the hope of glimpsing my friends. *Maybe I will be able to see better after most of the kids are sitting*, I think.

That turns out to be a very dumb thought, because I end up being one of the last kids standing. The giant is full-on yelling now, and I am pretty sure his eyes are locked on mine from a hundred feet away: "Just sit down! Anywhere! How hard can it be to put your butt in a chair?" I have just enough time to think, *Hey, that rhymes!* before a pair of hands grabs my shoulders and physically pushes me down into a seat. I look up and back and see that yet another massive mustache man is glaring at me from about six inches away.

"Eyes front!" he booms.

Doesn't anybody in this joint know how to use their inside voice?

I am at the edge of a row. Two boys next to me are snickering about something. One of the boys is incredibly pale and skinny, with gigantic glasses. He is wearing a bright green T-shirt and looks kind of like a praying mantis. The other boy is taller and looks much stronger, but he's also super pale.

As the guy onstage takes a loud, deep breath, the praying-mantis boy whispers, "How freaking pathetic is he?"

I turn toward them and say, "I know, right? And what's up with his walrus mustache? It looks like it's *alive*."

Mantis Boy hisses, "I'm not talking about *him*. I'm talking about *you*!"

I can't believe this. I have only been in this school for maybe four minutes, and I already have multiple enemies. At this rate, there are going to be WANTED posters of me in the bathrooms by lunchtime. I sigh, lean back in my seat, and settle in for a nice long lecture about how every sixth grader needs discipline, responsibility, maturity, and common sense.

Which is unfortunate, because I am not exactly famous for having any of those.

5. Another Life Tip, This One Regarding Reptiles

I have spent every summer since I was eight at Camp Lenape, my favorite place on earth. On a lake deep in the beautiful Pocono Mountains of Pennsylvania, camp is where I go to recover from all the trouble I get in during the school year. The main rules at Camp Lenape are "Shower at least once a week" and "Try not to die, especially on Visiting Day."

At camp, I have learned a lot of useful things, mostly by the experimentation method. Here's an example.

One of my favorite things about camp is all the wildlife. There are garter snakes everywhere you look, if you know what you are looking for and you move fast enough. You might see an occasional water snake in the lake, and there must theoretically be some copperheads and rattlesnakes in the woods somewhere, but I admit that nobody has ever seen any during my time at camp so far.

I don't give up hope, though.

I spend a lot of my time catching the garter snakes. It's tricky, because garters are quick. They are very sensitive to vibration, so you kind of have to tiptoe to get anywhere near them. Otherwise, they slither under a rock or a log, or even into the lake, before you can grab them. The grabbing part is also a challenge, because you have to pinch your fingers just behind the snake's head. If you don't, they can whip their bodies around and bite you.

This one time last summer, I was on my way up to the cabins after breakfast. I walked off the road a bit to see whether there were any snakes sunning themselves on this one big flat rock they like next to the edge of the tennis courts.

I was in luck! The biggest garter snake I have ever seen was fully exposed, basking in the warm sunlight. I snuck as close as I could without making a single sound. I was even holding my breath. I guess I wasn't quiet enough, though, because just as I got my hand close to its neck, the snake whipped around and sank its fangs into my right pointer finger.

Garter snake bites don't really hurt much, but they bleed, and you also have to get them cleaned out really well because any bite from a wild animal can give you an infection. As the snake let go of my finger, turned away, and disappeared under the edge of the rock, the two puncture wounds next to my fingernail started to well up with blood. I turned around and headed back toward the infirmary. The nurse, Mrs. Klemp, wasn't there, but Mrs. Kiely, one of the camp owners, was. Mrs. Kiely raised an eyebrow when she saw the snakebite, but didn't comment as she cleaned me up with a little bit of peroxide, a cotton ball, some triple antibiotic, and a Band-Aid.

On my way to my cabin again, I almost walked right by the tennis courts without looking at the big rock. But at this point, I thought, I was so late for cabin cleanup time that I might as well just take another moment to see whether the big snake was out again. It was! I couldn't believe the run of luck I was having.

In my defense, if it's hard catching a snake with your good hand, it's even harder doing it with your bad hand. And I'm a righty. Fifteen seconds later, my left thumb had two oozing puncture wounds. I headed back to the infirmary. This time, Mrs. Kiely saw me coming, and when I got within speaking range, she said one word: "Really?"

I might have been imagining it, but I felt like Mrs. Kiely was a bit less gentle during my second wound cleaning. When she finished, I had a Band-Aid on my right pointer and a big ball of gauze wrapped around my left thumb. "Now," she said, "go STRAIGHT BACK to your cabin, okay?"

"Okay," I mumbled. By this point, I was kind of sad. The biggest garter snake in the whole camp, and I had blown my chance at catching it—twice.

The famous jazz trumpeter Miles Davis once said that if you hit a wrong note, you should immediately play that note again so the audience thinks you did it on purpose. Mrs. Kiely must not be a big Miles Davis fan, because as the door slammed shut behind me, she snapped, "Jordan, you're a smart boy. Now *be smart*!"

That's not as easy as it sounds for a daredevil like

me. Sometimes, the smart move and the fun move are two different things. And I get them confused once in a while.

To tell you the truth, I get them confused daily. Sometimes even twice daily if there's a really cool snake involved.

By the way, I really hated it when she said that thing about being smart. When adults say you're smart, they are putting you under pressure. It's never just, "Hey, you're smart! Here's a nice cookie!" It's always, "You're smart! Can you demonstrate how to do this problem for the class?" Or "You're smart! Why don't you do better?" There is enough pressure on me to be smart even if nobody says a word, because all my adult relatives are super smart.

It's like if I am not smart, I should just get out of this family.

But then there's the problem of other kids. They hate it if you're too smart. Last year on report card day, I was at a friend's house after school. His mom looked at his report card, which had some Bs on it. Then she demanded to see my report card. I didn't know what to do, so I dug it out of my backpack and handed it over. I had all As. She turned to her son and said, "Why can't you be studious like Jordan?"

My friend gave me the dirtiest look I have ever received in my life. I rushed to say, "I'm not studious at all. I never study!"

So then his mom turned to him again and said, "Why can't you be smart like Jordan?"

I don't get invited over there anymore.

Being smart is like walking on a tightrope all the time. I have to keep getting almost everything right in school so I am not a disappointment to the family, but I also have to look like I don't try or care so the rest of the class doesn't hate me. It's exhausting.

I'd rather just have fun, even if it means getting bitten by a snake or two.

6. Lose a Tooth, Gain a Mortal Enemy (or Two)

In homeroom on the first day of sixth grade, I try to check out all the other kids without being too obvious about it. Geoff Straniere is in my homeroom, but Dougie Kaner isn't. We are in Homeroom 1A, and Dougie is in 1B across the hall. Even though Geoff and I should be next to each other in alphabetical order, I end up next to a boy named James Padilla, who is taller than I am, has his hair slicked back with a lot of product, and is wearing a shiny polyester dress shirt. On my other side is Joshua Stern, who is about my size and has very poofy hair and a big smile. My first thought is that he looks like a friendly cartoon character.

While I am chatting with James, I notice that the praying-mantis boy from assembly is directly in front of us. He is making snotty comments again, this time to a tall, pretty girl with very long brown hair. "Cookie," he says, "did you see how disorganized that assembly was? Seriously, this place is run by idiots."

I don't necessarily disagree, but his tone of voice is incredibly irritating.

"And," he continues, gesturing around the room with one hand, "what's the deal with the schedule? I can't believe we have to travel around together all day with *these* losers. To tell you the truth, I'm surprised there are this many kids in an A-track class that aren't even from P.S. 45."

Then he catches me and James staring at him, so he adds, "No offense."

"What's your name?" James asks him.

"Jimmy," he sneers. "Jimmy Ryan."

"Hi, Jiminy!" I say back with a big smile.

"It's not Jiminy, it's Jimmy."

"No," I say, "it's Jiminy. Because you look exactly like Jiminy Cricket."

"Oh, snap," James says under his breath.

"What's your problem?" Jimmy asks.

"I don't have a problem, Jiminy," I say. "Actually, I'm having a pretty good day so far, considering I'm a *pathetic loser*. But hey, at least my elementary school wasn't infested with crickets. No offense."

James is laughing beside me, and even the girl next to Jimmy is smiling. The bell rings before the argument can get totally out of hand, but Jimmy purposely bumps into my shoulder while I am waiting by the door for Geoff. It kind of hurts, because that's the same shoulder that slammed into the doorframe when I came into the building.

Swell, I think. *I definitely have my very first enemy of middle school. And my first bruise!*

I meet an even worse enemy moments later, when we arrive at the door of our English classroom. I am busy introducing James and Joshua to Geoff when the door opens and a weird-looking lady comes out. She looks like a character from a really old vampire movie. Her brittle-looking hair is pulled way back on her head so that the waxy skin of her face looks unnaturally tight. She is wearing the most makeup I have ever seen on a person who wasn't dead. Most of her face is super pale, but there is a circular area of bright pink on each cheek. She is wearing a white shirt that looks like it was made by stitching a bunch of white lace doilies together, a long tweed skirt, and black boots. She waves a hand at us, and I notice her finger-nails are creepily long.

"Line up against the wall!" she barks. "Silently!"

Apparently, she is a graduate of the Jimmy Ryan School of Making First Impressions.

When we are all in a row like toy soldiers, she waves her alarming nails in a strange, dismissing kind of motion. Nobody knows what she is trying to tell us, so we all just stare at her.

Finally, she huffs, "Well, come in! What are you waiting for—Christmas? We have work to accomplish!"

We file past her into the room, but then we are stuck again, because we don't have seat assignments. She makes us line up against the wall of the class. She seems to like lining us up against things. When we are all in, she says, "I am Miss Sarisky, your English language arts teacher. In *my* class, you will be seated in alphabetical order." For some reason, she says this with great pride, as though she has invented the concept of alphabetical seating.

As she seats the class, I listen to all the names, which I have already heard twice: once in the assembly while we were getting put into homerooms, and then again during attendance. The one other person I have met before, aside from Geoff, is Jennifer Deerfield, who was in my class from first grade through half of fourth, until I switched elementary schools. I smile at her as she sits down, and she smiles back. That makes me happy, because Jennifer is very nice and also very pretty.

The girl who was talking with Jimmy in homeroom is named Elizabeth Newgarden, not to be confused with a short blonde named Elizabeth Friedman. Elizabeth Friedman is not to be confused with a tall, thin blonde-haired girl named Elizabeth Maersh. Elizabeth Maersh is not to be confused with a tall, thin girl named Coty Metz, who has light brown hair and a merry smirk on her face. Or with another tall, thin blonde named Victoria Turvey, who is assigned to the seat next to me.

How am I supposed to keep track of who's who when nearly all the girls are tall and thin, and half of them are named Elizabeth?

There's a boy named Carlton Nalty, who has glasses like mine and also a perfectly shaped Afro. He is wearing a Beatles shirt. I instantly like him. I like anybody who likes the Beatles. Then there is a boy named Raymond Egan, who seems to be friends with Jimmy, and two other boys named Frankie and Kenny, who get scolded for talking to each other. There's also a very, very skinny boy with black-rimmed glasses and a briefcase. His name is Ben Bohen, and he looks like an extremely intelligent scarecrow. Finally, there's a tall, happy-looking boy named Ian Goldblum, who is sitting next to Jennifer Deerfield.

No wonder he looks so happy.

After I am seated, I learn that Jimmy's large cousin is named Michael Thompson. The last three kids to get seats are a girl named Carolyn Trifoglio, who has bright red hair; a girl named Shoshana Vogel, who is the tallest kid in the class; and a girl named Shanda Hernandez, who comes in late and gets the last open seat, two rows behind me.

Miss Sarisky starts lecturing us about boring stuff like how we are expected to set up our notebooks for her class. I know I should pay attention, but I get distracted by trying to look around the room and name all my classmates in my head. I am trying to come up with a clever way to memorize which Elizabeth is which when, all of a sudden, Miss Sarisky growls, "Isn't that right, *Jordan Sonnenblick?*"

On the bright side, at least the teacher is learning *my* name.

The rest of the school day goes smoothly, but that night during dinner, I bite down wrong on a piece of meat and feel a shocking crunch as blood fills my mouth. My right canine tooth, which is the last baby tooth I have, is suddenly loose. This is excellent! I love having a loose tooth, because Lissa taught me from a very young age how to gross people out by wiggling your tooth and twisting it into weird positions. I have a feeling this tooth won't be around for long, though. I must be a hard chewer, because with one hard bite, I have practically ripped it out of my head.

The next morning is bad. When I wake up, I feel like a giant is sitting on my chest. I am having an asthma attack. Fortunately, my mom is constantly stashing inhalers all over the house, and there is one on the bookshelf above my head. I grab it, suck in a couple of puffs, and feel my chest open up. Unfortunately, I also feel my heart start to pound and my hands and feet begin to shake.

Using my asthma medicines always makes me feel shaky, jumpy, and kind of twitchy all over. This is a problem, because I have trouble paying attention and behaving on my best days. When I am on my meds, there's basically no chance I won't get busted for something during the day.

Now, I could go downstairs, tell my mother I woke up all tight and wheezy, and get a free day off from school. But then she would take me to the doctor, who would put me on even worse medicines and make me stay home for a whole week. There's no way I can miss the next five days of school— by the time I get back, everyone will have already made all their friends, and I will be an outcast for the next three years.

Not an option.

So instead, I sneak into the medicine cabinet in my parents' bathroom and find the bottle of Theo-Dur. Theo-Dur is like super-caffeine. It makes my heart pound even worse than the inhaler does. It also causes my legs to shiver so much that I know I will have muscle cramps for days after I take it. But I also know that if I take the Theo-Dur, I can go to school and probably not die. I have trouble opening the childproof cap of the bottle with my hands already shaking from the inhaler, but eventually it pops off. I try to pour out just one of the little football-shaped pills, but of course, a torrent of them pours out. There are pills on the counter, pills on the floor, pills in the sink. There's even a pill in the toilet. I scoop up all the ones I can find, swallow one, flush the toilet to get rid of the evidence, and head for the kitchen.

I figure I'll get through the day, no problem.

This time, I manage to enter the school without smashing into the doors, so that's a plus. My shoulder is a fairly horrifying shade of purple from yesterday's collisions, and I've got enough other stuff to worry about. When we are all at our lockers before homeroom, I hunch way down with my head nearly crammed into mine to take another puff on my inhaler without anybody seeing. I have a bottom locker, right under Joshua's, so as long as nobody kneels down and stares right at me, I should be able to sneak the puff without being observed.

We're supposed to sign all our medications in with the nurse, but if I do that, then I will have to go to her whenever I feel tight. Then she will have to call my mom every time, and I will never make it through a full week of school.

My pediatrician, Dr. Purow, says that the goal of asthma management is to keep the patient well controlled. Sadly, asthma is yet another area of life in which I am, as they say in the asthma business, poorly controlled. You're not supposed to have to rely on your rescue inhaler more than once in a rare while. I have already done three puffs before eight a.m.

Well, breathing is overrated, I say. I shove my inhaler back into the front pocket of my backpack. Just as I am about to close my locker and stand up, some kid nudges me from behind so that the top of my head comes up against the sharp bottom edge of Joshua's open locker door. It hurts, and I'm pretty sure my scalp might actually be bleeding, but I can't go to the nurse, because if she notices that my hands are shaking or that my heart is pounding about a hundred and ten times a minute, the whole asthma cycle will get fired up and I will be out of here.

Trying hard not to rub my head, I walk slowly into class just in time to get marked present. So that's a win.

James and Joshua chat across me all through homeroom, but I don't say much. Between the Theo-Dur, the inhaler, and the throbbing that has started up in my gashed head, I feel like I am about to jump out of my skin. I distract myself by using my tongue to play with my loose tooth, which is already barely hanging on by a thread.

By the way, I kind of like the taste of blood. I wonder whether that is weird.

I let myself get swept along as my class moves to first period as one big pack. We line up outside of the door like Miss Sarisky told us to. And then something comes over me. It's part idea, part impulse. I will show Miss Sarisky my loose tooth!

When she steps into the doorway and does her odd fingernail-sweep thing to tell us to come in, the line surges forward. When I am almost directly in front of her, I smile as big as I can and say, "Hi, Miss Sa-ritthhh-key!" while pushing my tooth outward with my tongue. My goal is just to make the tooth flip upward and outward, but I guess I am too pumped up, because the tooth pops out of my mouth completely and goes flying at my

new teacher. It bounces off her neck, leaving a very visible dot of blood on her chalky skin, and *falls down the front of her shirt.*

I stop short. All the kids behind me bang into each other like dominoes. Miss Sarisky starts screaming at the top of her lungs. She is yelling so fast that I only catch a few parts:

"*Wrong* with you?"

"So disrespectful!"

"I have never!"

"Disgusting!"

"Germs!"

And, finally, "OFFICE!"

I feel kind of numb as I step out of the line and turn around. For a second, I find myself face-to-face with Jimmy Ryan. "Nice job!" he says.

I don't even know where the office is. All I can think as I stumble down the silent, empty hall is that I should have stayed in bed. Or at least asked Miss Sarisky for my tooth back. This is going to be a tough one to explain to the tooth fairy.

7. Pick Your Heroes Carefully, Part II

Evel Knievel has kept me in danger for many years now. Two of my other heroes, Spider-Man and John Lennon, have kept me in trouble. See, here's the thing about Spider-Man and John Lennon: They both started out as smart, nerdy guys with glasses—like me! Then they magically transformed into powerful, wisecracking, defiant, *famous* smart, nerdy guys. They didn't have to change who they were inside in order to become larger than life. Spider-Man is still Peter Parker, shy science genius, under his mask. He can climb up walls and beat up bad guys, but he also invented his own web fluid formula along with the wrist shooters he uses to fire the webs. John Lennon became the leader of the most famous rock group in the history of the world—the Beatles—but he also wrote and published two really strange, funny little books full of jokes, poetry, cartoons, and general wackiness. Then he quit the band, because *John Lennon doesn't care what anybody thinks.*

The wisecracking part is maybe the most important thing of all to me. Peter Parker casually makes jokes even when he's right in the middle of fighting bad guys. Like this one time, a villain named Electro sees him coming and shouts, "SPIDER-MAN!" Spider-Man replies, "I'm glad you remembered the hyphen! Most people leave it out!"

That's funny.

And John Lennon once made fun of the Queen of England right to her face. The Beatles were playing a concert for the Queen, and all her rich friends were sitting in the front rows of the theater. John said to the audience, "The people in the cheaper seats, clap your hands. And the rest of you, if you'd just rattle your jewelry." The best part is that, when he said it, the Queen waved and smiled.

That's funny and defiant!

I feel like if I can just figure out their tricks, I'll be cool. I've got the smart-nerd-with-glasses part down already. The problem is the transformation part. I haven't met any radioactive spiders lately, or even Paul, George, or Ringo. So I spend a lot of time trying to make my own defiant, wisecracking magic.

Like this one time in fifth grade, my homeroom—Class 5-317—was in the library. Two of my friends, Mark Anderson and Doug Friedman, were flipping baseball cards, which is basically like playing War, except with a stack of valuable collector's items instead of a deck of playing cards. Mark and Doug must each have had at least a hundred and fifty cards to draw from, and there was a huge pile growing on the tile floor between them, when, suddenly, the shadow of our scary librarian, Mrs. Rainbow, fell over our little group.

I know that you don't picture someone frightening when you hear the name "Mrs. Rainbow," but this lady was shockingly tough. Without saying a word, she bent down and scooped up all the cards in the pile. Then she held out her other hand for Mark and Doug to give her all the cards that hadn't been on the floor. Still without saying anything, she walked away and put all the cards in the drawer behind the counter.

First Mark went up to Mrs. Rainbow and asked politely for the cards back. Mrs. Rainbow barely looked at him. Then I walked over with Doug and watched him totally beg her for the cards. He was practically crying, but all Mrs. Rainbow did was shake her head. I couldn't stand it. I said, "You can't just take their cards away. It's not against the school rules to have baseball cards."

"In this library," she said, "I *make* the rules." Then she turned her back on us.

Nobody turns their back on Spider-Man. John Lennon. Jordan Sonnenblick. Whatever. You know what I'm saying. I hate when something is unfair, and I hate it even more when a grown-up pushes a kid around just because she *can*.

I called a meeting of my class's library helpers. There were maybe eight of us who stayed in during recess or came to the library after school and helped shelve the books, neaten things up, and do whatever else needed to be done. Doug and I were both part of the group, but Mrs. Rainbow hadn't cared whether we had helped her a thousand times. She hadn't let that stop her from stealing Doug's stuff and disrespecting me.

I said to the other helpers, "Listen, we are the Class 5-317 Library Squad, right?"

Everybody nodded.

"And a squad is a group, right? Like a team?"

They nodded again.

"And when somebody hurts a member of our team, do we just sit and watch, or do we defend our friend?"

They all just looked at me.

"Doug," I asked, "what do you think?"

"We, uh, defend our friend?"

"That's right!" I said. "Are you all with me?"

More stares.

"ARE YOU ALL WITH ME?" I practically shouted.

"YEAH!" Doug yelled. A few of the other kids mumbled things that sounded kind of like agreement, so I kept going.

"Now, here's the plan: We, the members of the Class 5-317 Library Squad, are officially on strike, for as long as it takes to get Doug and Mark's cards back. We can make posters that say, uh, something like:

THE 5-317 LIBRARY SQUAD IS ON STRIKE!
FOR LIBERTY!
FOR JUSTICE!
FOR BASEBALL CARDS!"

"Ooh, that's good," Doug said.

"Thanks, Doug," I replied. "Now, are we all in?"

Nobody said no. And that was the beginning of our devastating three-week strike. The other kids all stopped showing up at the library.

But not me. I was our mole inside the system. I was the only one who kept going to the library at volunteer time. I wrote our slogan on dozens of index cards and plain old sheets of loose-leaf paper. Every time I shelved a book, I hid one of our declarations inside it. This went on for weeks without Mrs. Rainbow seeming to notice anything was going on. But then one day, when our teacher, Mr. Lord, was in the middle of reading us a chapter from this amazing book called *The Count of Monte Cristo*, she knocked on our classroom door.

Well, really it was more like she *banged* on our classroom door.

Mr. Lord put the book down, walked over to her, and listened for a couple of minutes as she whispered furiously, waving her hands all over the place. She even slapped a pile of my index cards down on the chalkboard ledge, making dust fly everywhere. Until that moment, I hadn't realized a librarian could *get* that mad. But wow, Mrs. Rainbow was enraged.

So was Mr. Lord. He turned to the class and gave this whole speech about honor and dignity, and how we had disgraced his name.

Which wasn't even true. It's not like his name was 5-317. But even I was smart enough not to point that out.

Then Mr. Lord dropped the bomb. Our class would be

staying inside for recess every day for a week unless somebody told him who had been behind this disgraceful display of disrespect.

For a while nobody said anything. Doug, Mark, and I exchanged glances. Doug and I sat directly across a table from each other. Doug nodded at me. I nodded at him. He wrote on a little scrap of paper and passed it to a girl named Linda Sterlacci, who passed it to me. I read it and mouthed, "Okay. One. Two. Three!"

Then Doug and I stood up, slammed in our chairs, and said, "We did it! We did it and we're *proud*!"

It was a completely epic moment. But my friends never got their cards back, Doug and I missed the week of recess while everyone else got to play, and Mr. Lord spent the rest of the year thinking we were delinquents.

It's almost like I don't have this whole nerd-hero thing figured out yet.

8. You Can't Just Go to Any Old Office

I wander the halls for a while, feeling sorry for myself. My mouth is bleeding, the scab on my head and the bruise on my shoulder both ache, and my heart is pounding from the combination of trouble and Theo-Dur. Finally, I stumble upon a door with a big sign over it that says MAIN OFFICE. I take a deep breath, which causes me to have a coughing fit, and then push open the door.

"What are you here for, young man?" the secretary says.

I have an 8:45 haircut appointment, I almost say. *What do you think I'm here for, lady? I'm here to get yelled at.*

"Um, Miss Sarisky sent me?"

"She sent you *here*?"

"Well, she told me to go to the office."

"Why did she send you to *this* office?"

Uh, because the office of I.S. 27 would be too far to walk? "She didn't tell me which office to go to. She just said to go to the office. I didn't ask which one. I didn't even know there were choices."

The secretary literally rolls her eyes at me, which honestly is just hurtful. Then she looks down at a paper taped to her desk. I'm pretty sure she mutters, "Ugh, sixth graders!" under her breath. When she looks back up at me, she says, "You're on team 6-1, right?"

I have no idea what team I am on. Until this very moment, I hadn't even known I was on a team. All I know is that my team doesn't seem to be winning.

I stare at her blankly.

She sighs and says, "What homeroom are you in?"

Okay, that's a question I can actually answer. "I'm in 1A."

"That means you're on team 6-1. Mr. Overbye is your assistant principal. His office is upstairs, on the second floor. Do you know how to get to the second floor?"

Yes, I am pretty sure I know how to use a staircase for ascending purposes.

"I think so."

"Okay, let me just call and let him know you're coming. What's your name?"

"Jordan Sonnenblick."

She dials. "Hi, Steve? It's Terri. I'm sending a student up. His name is . . . uh, Jason Solomon-X?"

"Actually, it's Jordan Sonnenblick."

"Jordan Slobber-Neck?"

"Okay, fine," I say. "Just tell him it's Joe Smith." I grab a hard candy from a basket on the counter, turn, and walk out.

I like the taste of hard candy. I like the taste of blood. But sadly, it turns out that I hate the two tastes at once. I guess that's why they don't make Reese's Hard Candy and Blood Cups. Some great tastes don't taste great together.

I find the stairwell, trudge up to the second floor, and start roaming around looking for an office. Eventually, I come to a door with a placard that says THOMAS STEVEN OVERBYE. Looking in through the little window in the door, I see a tiny waiting room and then an inner office. The world's largest, reddest man is staring at me from behind a desk. He is practically too big for his chair. It looks like if he stood up quickly, his legs would shatter the desk and his head would smash through the drop ceiling. His hair is a reddish-blond,

and there is a lot of it, including the bushiest mustache I have ever seen in my life. His face looks like he's just done fifty push-ups.

He looks like a Viking. An angry Viking.

He raises one ham-sized arm and waves me in.

I take a seat facing him across the desk.

"Are you Jordan Sonnenblick?" he asks.

I nod.

"What took you so long to GET here?" he asks, randomly emphasizing the word *GET*.

I'm like, *Well, first I had to do preschool and kindergarten. Then there was first grade, second grade, third grade* . . . But I am terrified, so I simply say, "I got lost."

He takes a deep breath and leans back in his chair with his hands crossed on his stomach. "I got off the phone with your English teacher a few minutes ago. She says you spat your tooth out at her. Do you want to tell me *exactly what you were THINKING*?"

I never understand why grown-ups ask this. When they were kids, did they go around *thinking* all the time before they did stupid things? Really?

"Well, my tooth was loose . . ."

"CLEARly."

"But I didn't know it was *that* loose. I just wanted to show off how loose it was, and then . . . before I knew it . . ."

"Your tooth was bouncing off your teacher's NECK and down her SHIRT?"

I shrug. "Well, basically."

He sighs. "Listen, Jordan. We are going to be spending the next three years together. They can be very easy, short years, or they can be very DIFFICULT, LONG years. That is your choice. Wouldn't you rather have three EASY years?"

Duh.

I nod.

"Then here is what is going to happen. You are going to go downstairs and APOLOGIZE to Miss Sarisky. Can you do that?"

I hate apologizing, especially for things I didn't even do on purpose, but I force myself to nod.

"And can you promise me you won't do this AGAIN?"

Well, at least that's an easy one. I nod. I don't have any more baby teeth.

I have missed all of Miss Sarisky's class, so I head straight to second period, which is band. Having band second period is actually pretty impressive for a sixth grader, because the I.S. 61 Morning Band is a famous thing. The kids who don't do well in their band auditions at the end of fifth grade get put in the afternoon band, which doesn't even get to perform in concerts. It's like the minor leagues.

The Morning Band is definitely not the minor leagues. Not only do we get to perform a lot, but we get special red blazer jackets to wear on performance days. Peter Friedman says that if you're wearing a red band blazer, you don't even have to go to class. You can hang out in the band room, which is just the stage with the curtain closed. And if a teacher stops you in the hallway and asks you why you aren't in class, you can point to your red blazer. It's not just an item of clothing; it's a hall pass made of shiny polyester.

The blazer is so important that yesterday we spent the second half of the period getting individually measured for them by some old lady while the band teacher, Mr. Impolito, called sixth graders into his office in the back corner of the stage one by one and made us play. The kids who play horns or woodwinds had to play scales. We drummers had to show Mr. Impolito our rudiments. The rudiments are these special exercises drummers do in order to develop good technique. And just like any song's melody is actually made up of notes from scales, each song's drum parts are made up of rudiments.

I am good at rudiments. I have been taking lessons since fourth grade, and my teacher, Mr. Stoll, is very serious about technique.

I am not so good at what we did the first half of the period, which was listen to Mr. Impolito's big first-day speech about The Proud Tradition of the Morning Band. His speech was kind of like a piece of classical music. It started out quiet, with him saying things like, "I have been a professional musician for over twenty-five years. My trumpet and I have gone off to the army together. We've seen the world. And now we are back where we started, teaching music to the next generation." Then it got louder and louder, and he got more and more into it, so that he was sweating visibly and his greasy hair was actually flopping around as he talked about "dignity" and "respect" and how each of us would be expected to "honor the jacket."

Unfortunately, this made me and my fellow new drummer, Coty Metz, giggle. I mean, I wasn't trying to be bad, but honestly, how in the world do you honor a jacket? Is there a prayer to the jacket? A sacred vow? Some kind of elaborate jacket-related ritual?

Once Coty and I got started with the laughing, we couldn't stop. Carlton Nalty joined in, too. Our section leader, a very serious eighth grader named Andrew Seligman, tried to shush us, but that just made it worse. By the time Mr. Impolito reached the roaring climax of his speech, Andrew was actually kicking us in the ankles in an attempt to restore order.

Mr. Impolito noticed.

When he called me into his office to play, I got through all my rudiments perfectly. The flam, the ratamacue, the double flam, the flam tap, the paradiddle, the five-, seven-, and nine-stroke rolls—I nailed everything. When I stopped playing, Mr. Impolito stared at me through his thick brown-framed glasses and said, "Well, the playing is there. But the comportment needs work. Do you know what I mean by comportment, Sonnenblick?"

It just so happened I did know. I read a lot. "Do you mean my behavior, my bearing, how I carry myself?"

Mr. Impolito smiled a thin, painful-looking kind of smile

and said, "Very good, Sonnenblick. Now get out of here and send Metz in."

Sometimes a grown-up says "very good," but you know they're really saying, "I don't like you."

Anyway, by the time I get from Mr. Overbye's office to the band room, the late bell has already rung. You have to walk up a half flight of stairs to get up to stage level from the hall-way, and as my head comes up above the level of the railing, Mr. Impolito is about to start conducting warm-up scales. He sees me and mouths, "You're late. Get in here!"

I have to walk around the back of the entire band to get to where the drum section is, which is embarrassing. All the band kids who are in my homeroom, like two of the three Elizabeths, Shoshana, a girl named Joanna Ramsey, and Jimmy Ryan, turn to stare at me. I don't blame them. I am the first member of our class to get sent to the office, and the last time they saw me, I was spitting my upper right canine tooth at our English teacher. Most of the kids look kind of concerned. Jimmy is smirking.

Geoff, who is sitting behind the drum line with a pair of sticks in his hands, gives me a thumbs-up. Carlton, who is playing the bass drum, nods at me. Coty is standing behind Andrew Seligman, watching him play the snare drum. I stand behind the other snare drummer, a seventh-grade girl named Lisa, which puts me next to Coty.

"So, what happened?" Coty whispers.

"I had to see this guy named Mr. Overbye."

"Wow, you saw *The Bee*? Shoshana's big brother, Duane, told us he's horrifying. Did you get in big trouble?"

"No," I say. "I just had to promise not to do that again."

Coty smiles. "Do that again? How many loose teeth does he think you *have*?"

This makes me snort. Uh-oh.

Mr. Impolito sees. He cuts off the band. "Sonnenblick, while I am gratified that you have decided to grace us with your presence, I am less than thrilled with your attitude. Listen, son, I need to know something: Are you a musician, or are you a clown?"

Clearly, this is a trick question. If I say I'm a musician, then he will say, "Then why are you acting like a clown?" But if I say I'm a clown, he'll yell at me for *that*.

The answer comes to me in a flash! "Um, a little of both?"

My band teacher slides his glasses down his nose, glares at me over the top of the frames, and says, "Sonnenblick, go to the office!"

Two times in two periods. It's like the snakebite incident all over again.

Oh well, I think as I walk back across the stage with everybody's eyes on me. *At least now I know* which *office*.

9. The Problem with Being a Legend

By the end of the first few weeks of school, I am strangely famous. I am That Kid Who Gets Sent to The Bee's Office All the Time. I'm the kid who keeps things interesting in Miss Sarisky's boring class. I'm the class rebel. It's not like I asked for this job. But hey, somebody's got to do it.

In my defense, I don't go looking for trouble. It just finds me. Like with Miss Sarisky. Apparently, she spent the whole period I missed on the second day of school lecturing the class about her Number One Rule: TAKE DETAILED, ACCURATE NOTES! Which is a dumb rule, if you ask me.

First of all, I don't even believe that is her Number One Rule. Obviously, her real Number One Rule is DON'T SPIT YOUR TOOTH OUT AT MY NECK! Second of all, I learn better if I am looking at the teacher, not trying to take "detailed, accurate notes." In fact, I don't even know how to take "detailed, accurate notes." I have major penmanship problems, so I write pretty slowly. This means that I can't write down everything Miss Sarisky says, or I fall way behind. But if I try to just write down the important things, I don't write anything—because nothing this woman says is important.

The result is that Miss Sarisky is constantly yelling at me about *The Pitiful State of Your Notebook, Jordan Sonnenblick.* We have quizzes every week on spelling, vocabulary, and reading comprehension. I get every single item right, every single time. One day I say to her when she is yelling at me about my pitiful notebook for the thousandth time, "Why should I write all this stuff down in my notebook if I don't need it to get a hundred on every quiz?"

So what does Miss Sarisky do? Does she leave me alone because I am right? No, she starts collecting our notebooks every Friday and grading them.

This is particularly unfortunate for Coty and Geoff, who have been drawing cartoon Miss Sarisky figures all over the margins of their notebook pages. The cartoons are not flattering. To be fair, though, they *are* detailed and accurate.

Geoff, Coty, and I spend a lot of time trying not to make eye contact in Miss Sarisky's class, because if we do, we start laughing. And if we start laughing, it spreads to Shoshana, Joanna, and Joshua. Sometimes, the spread continues until the entire class is giggling. Well, except for Jimmy Ryan. Jimmy usually just rolls his eyes and mutters, "Real mature, morons!" under his breath.

In band, we are finding other ways to get in trouble. Again, this isn't totally our fault. Our section leader, Andrew, is constantly on us. I'm pretty sure he feels threatened because Coty reads music better than he does and my rolls are at least as good as his. Plus, Mr. Impolito is constantly giving us the Evil Eye and making comments. It's embarrassing enough getting corrected in a normal class with thirty other kids. In a band class with like seventy kids, it's much worse. Mr. Impolito frequently cuts off the entire band and says, "Would you like to share the joke with us, Sonnenblick?"

It only takes me two tries to learn that the correct answer is "No."

And of course, I am bursting with energy all day from my asthma meds. I am probably having the worst asthma month of my life. My allergist has put me on a twenty-day course of steroids, which means I feel like I am going to jump out of my skin at any moment.

It doesn't help that I sit between Coty and Geoff whenever we aren't playing. When we are playing, Coty and I are usually next to each other. Coty has an extremely unnerving habit of bumping her hip against me while we are playing in order to get my attention.

It works.

Sometimes, I get so distracted by Coty's hip touching mine that I lose my place in the music. Or I stop playing. Or, worst of all, I play a bunch of wrong notes, causing the dreaded Impolito Cutting Off The Band Effect.

If the hip bump itself doesn't mess me up, looking over at

Coty's face does. She isn't exactly beautiful like Jennifer Deerfield or Elizabeth Newgarden or Joanna Ramsey. She doesn't have curves yet, like Shoshana does. But she has flashing eyes, a grin bursting with the promise of mischief, and a laugh that makes me feel like I have accomplished a daring top-secret mission every time I cause it.

Sometimes, when we are all sitting down and the other sections are tuning up and running through their scales, Coty picks up her sticks and plays rudiments on the top of my leg. After a while, I start playing on hers, too. It's usually hard to play on soft surfaces because you can't get the right bounce. But Coty's jeans are so tight I can play a flawless buzz roll on them.

She knows every Beatles song I do. She often says exactly what I am thinking before I say it. And she does a perfect Jimmy Ryan impression.

I think I am hypnotized or something. Geoff thinks I am in love.

One thing's for sure. Romance is not good for my conduct. Or, as Vinny Impolito would say, my comportment.

Geoff says Coty is flirting with me. I am pretty sure this has never happened to me before, so I don't have much to compare it to. But I have a feeling he may be right. Geoff tells me I should ask her out. So do Shoshana and Joanna. I know I can't stop thinking of her and all, but asking a girl out is a big step for me. A really big step. Like, Neil Armstrong stepping on the surface of the moon big.

If she says no, I will be disgraced forever. Coty's friends will look at me and giggle. My friends will make rude remarks. Jimmy Ryan will have a field day.

On the other hand, if she says yes, Coty's friends will look at me and giggle. My friends will make rude remarks. And Jimmy Ryan will have a field day. Plus, then I will actually have to go out with a real girl. On a real date. I have no idea what that even means. Am I supposed to pick her up on my bicycle and pedal her to Pal Joey's, our local pizza restaurant? Or take the city bus? A taxi?

Speaking of the city bus, that's how I get home from school three days a week, when my mom is working late. I walk from the school to the corner of Forest Avenue and Victory Boulevard, which is nearly a mile away, with Shoshana, Joanna, and Shoshana's big brother, Duane. Shoshana and Joanna are trying to convince me to make the big move on Coty, and I tell them how stupid I will feel trying to transport us somewhere. Duane says it is totally acceptable for my mom to drive us to a date, "as long as she doesn't speak."

Duane has never met my mom.

Duane, Shoshana, and Joanna get into a heated discussion over where I should go with Coty. Which is annoying because I haven't even asked her yet. Plus, even if I do ask her, AND she says yes, AND my mom agrees to drive us in silence, there's the problem of what one actually does on a date. What am I supposed to wear? Am I supposed to put on some kind of boy perfume? What will we talk about? What if she wants to hold hands? What if my palms are sweaty? What if she wants to kiss?

What if she *doesn't* want to kiss?

The more my friends talk about this, the more overwhelming the whole mission seems. Like D-Day. But at least before D-Day, the soldiers had training. I don't know *anything*. I will probably freeze up completely. Probably I should just hand Coty a stuffed animal of some sort and let her go on a date with *that*. She would probably have more fun.

In spite of me, the whole thing somehow gets decided. I will ask Coty to go roller-skating with me at Skate Odyssey, two Saturdays from now. Here's how it will work: I will pass a note to Geoff. Geoff will pass the note to Shoshana (or Joanna), who will pass it to Coty, who will write YES or NO on it. Then Coty will pass the note back to Shoshana (or Joanna), who will pass it back to Geoff (or possibly Joshua), who will pass it back to me.

That is six note-passings. It seems to me that there is a significant risk of interception. But apparently, my input is not necessary. The plan is the plan. My only job is to write the note.

I work on it all night, and it is a masterpiece. It says, and I quote, *Coty, will you go to Skate Odyssey with me?* Under that, there are two boxes, one for YES and one for NO. Hopefully, Coty will check the YES box. I illustrate the margins with pictures of drumsticks, the logos of bands, and a heart. But then I worry that a heart might be too mushy, so I change that into a baseball. I have no idea why I choose a baseball, because as far as I can remember, Coty and I have never even discussed baseball. I almost rip the note up and start again, but I really like the way the Beatles and AC/DC logos look, so I fold it up as neatly as I can, write *FROM: Jordan S.* on one side and *TO: Coty M.* on the other, and stick it into my English notebook.

Why my English notebook? Because I don't want to get in trouble with my social studies teacher, Mr. Bretstein, who is incredibly cool; my math teacher, Mrs. Lee, who is super patient and really good at explaining things; or my science teacher, Mr. Gallo, who is best friends with Mr. Overbye. I can't do it in band, because Coty would be right next to me. That would be incredibly awkward if she says no. Gym is out, because how would that even work? And my only other class is Spanish with Señora Gutilla. Coty takes French.

Of course, the English thing is a problem because Miss Sarisky watches me every second like she is a hawk and I am a mouse she particularly hates. There's no way I can pass the note in her class without getting busted instantly. So, when everybody is lining up outside her door the next day, I give the note to Victoria Turvey, who sits next to me, and ask her to pass it across the room.

This was not the plan. I was supposed to just hand the note to Geoff. From there, the whole passing chain was already supposed to be worked out. But I am too nervous to wait all day to get my answer, and English is our first class. Also, I feel embarrassed handing the note to Geoff, for some reason. He is super popular and good-looking. He even has a girlfriend from his old private school. They have been going out since before the summer! That is more than three months!

Geoff must think I am such an amateur.

If he does think that, he is right. My decision is SO DUMB! Vicky and I sit all the way across the room from Coty, plus we sit in the third row from the front, and Coty sits all the way in the back. If I was going to ditch the original plan, why didn't I give the note before class to Elizabeth Maersh, who sits two seats in front of Coty? Or Elizabeth Newgarden, who sits just one row over from Coty?

Or even possibly to someone whose name isn't Elizabeth?

But once Vicky has the note, all I can do is wait. And sweat.

Vicky reaches across the aisle and passes the note to Raymond Egan, who slips it to Carlton Nalty while Miss Sarisky is writing on the board. Then Miss Sarisky tells us to take out our homework from last night. As people are shuffling around their papers and Miss Sarisky is walking across the room to the first row, Carlton flips the note to Elizabeth Maersh. Elizabeth holds on to the note until Miss Sarisky gets distracted by a call over the intercom. Then Liz slips the note over her shoulder to Liz Newgarden, who coughs to get Michael Thompson's attention. Liz drops the note on the floor by Michael's feet. Then Miss Sarisky takes forever going over the homework answers while the sweat drips slowly down my forehead into my eyes. It's ridiculous. I have literally never been this nervous.

By the time Michael hands the note to Coty, the period is almost over.

I am dying. Coty glances over to me, and I have to assume she wonders why my entire head is soaked with sweat. I must look like I just fell off the Staten Island Ferry. But I force myself to smile at her. Hopefully that will distract her from the fact that I am slowly drowning in the middle of English class.

Then disaster strikes. The bell rings.

Now I have to sit next to Coty in band before I have an answer.

But that's not the worst thing. Apparently, everybody has noticed the whole note-passing saga, because I can hear people whispering about it as we leave the room and start walking up the hallway. Jimmy Ryan is right behind me, asking his cousin Michael Thompson, "Who on earth would go out with *Jordan*?"

I don't know whether to hurry to band so I can get away from the whispers or slow down so I don't have to face Coty yet. I stop at a water fountain and take the longest drink in the history of I.S. 61, which is probably a smart move with all the fluids I have been losing. But even this mighty drink can't last forever, and eventually I have to head off to the stage with my stomach sloshing.

Most of the band is already sitting, and I feel like the eyes of all the people from my homeroom are glued to me. I sit down between Geoff and Coty and pray that, no matter what Coty's answer is, I don't cry or faint in the middle of the drum line. I stare straight ahead at Mr. Impolito for what feels like a million years, although really it can't be that long because the flutes are in the middle of a scale when I feel Coty's elbow in my ribs.

I look her in the eye. She is holding the note. She has that Coty grin going as she says, "So. Nice note."

I can't breathe. "Uh, yeah. About that. I don't know . . . I don't mean to, uh . . . you don't have to answer it if you don't . . . uh, want to."

Wow, I think. *I sure do say "uh" a lot when I am panicking.*

Coty slaps the note into my hand. "Jordan, you goofball. Yes!"

As Coty and I are walking out of the band room together, I am feeling kind of happy and kind of terrified, both at once. If this is love, I am going to need to make a serious investment in deodorant products. Then Jimmy Ryan slides up behind us and says, "Oh, *now* I know who would go out with you, Jordan. Coty! That figures."

He says *Coty* the way most people would say *rotting pig guts*.

I turn and push him. He pushes me back. Geoff, Joshua, Michael Thompson, and a couple of other kids get between us. "We'll settle this after school," Geoff hisses at Michael. "After school," Michael spits back.

"Playground fence?" Geoff asks.

"Playground fence," Mike replies. "Jimmy will be there!"

Great! This is what having a reputation does for you. Now I suddenly have plans for a date *and* a fight.

I'm not sure which one is scarier.

10. Pick Your Heroes Carefully, the Threequel

My Grandpa Sol's first memory is from when he was a kid back in Poland, before his family fled to America and settled on the Lower East Side of Manhattan. He was only six when he got to New York, so he must have been really little when this story happened.

In his area, near the border of Russia, all the Jews lived in isolated towns called shtetls. The center of the shtetl was the temple, and the rabbi was more than just the leader of the temple's services. He was also the teacher for all the kids. Anyway, one day on the walk to the temple for school, my grandfather got distracted by a little kitten that was meowing from under a bridge over a stream. My grandfather climbed down, got the kitten away from the water, and played with it for a while. Then he suddenly realized he would be late to class, so he put down the kitten and ran the rest of the way.

When my grandfather got to school, the rabbi was furious. I guess teachers in Europe were pretty terrifying, because he grabbed a whip and told my grandfather—a five-year-old— that he was going to give him a beating for coming to school late. Grandpa Sol did the smartest thing he could: He jumped through an open window and ran home.

According to my grandpa's story, the rabbi chased him all the way.

When they both arrived at my great-grandparents' little house, my grandfather ran past his parents and hid behind my Great-Grandma Jenny. The rabbi, still holding his whip, ordered her to hand my grandpa over so he could be punished. My Great-Grandpa Louis, who was apparently not super nice, turned to Great-Grandma Jenny and told her to hand my grandpa over. Great-Grandma Jenny turned to the rabbi and said, "If you want to get to my kid, first you have to get through me."

My grandpa has always been pretty vague about how that whole affair turned out, but that's not really the point. What I have always taken from that story is that you don't have to let anybody push you around, no matter who they are. My grandpa and his mom were old-school rebels. He jumped out the window and ran home! She stood up to the rabbi, the most important guy in town.

Sure enough, my grandfather brought that kind of tough stubbornness to America, where he eventually passed it on to me. Even now, as an old man, he always insists on carrying all the luggage when there's a family trip, and he is unbelievably strong. He's also fearless. I guess if you have enough guts to jump out a window and run away from school when you're five, everything else seems like a piece of cake.

Grandpa was a high school biology teacher until he retired, and he also wrote a bunch of science articles and even a couple of textbooks. What he really loves, though, is getting out into nature and seeing animals up close. Once, when I was visiting him in Florida, he took me and my sister, Lissa, out on an airboat tour in the Everglades. He made sure he had the seat next to the water, with me right next to him. When the boat stopped next to a massive alligator, my grandfather grabbed me under the armpits, lifted me up across his lap, and tilted my whole body so that my face was way over the edge of the boat, maybe two feet above the alligator.

"Are you close enough?" he asked me in his booming voice.

I was too terrified to answer.

Luckily, Lissa shouted, "He's close enough! He's close enough!"

Another time, I was chasing a lizard behind my grandparents' condominium, and it ran under a log next to the canal that's back there. I lifted the log and found myself face-to-face with a cottonmouth water moccasin, which was bad because water moccasins are venomous and also have very bad tempers. Just as the snake began to strike at me, I jumped back and dropped the log, which pinned him down so that only his

head and the front six inches of his body were sticking out. His mouth was open, and I could see his fangs and the white lining of his mouth.

I ran upstairs and got my grandpa, who came down and beat the snake nearly to death with a sharp stick. But the stick kept breaking until it was just a little stub in his hands. Workers were installing sewer pipes across the little walkway by the canal, and one of the guys came over to us and started smashing the snake with a piece of white plastic pipe. That shattered, too, but then the man brought its jagged edge down and chopped the front of the snake off completely.

By this point, I was feeling pretty creeped out. But my grandfather said, "This is great! Now we can examine the specimen!" He got two new sticks and used them to pinch and lift the front six inches of the snake like it was the world's grossest noodle. "Bend down close, Jordan! Notice how the inside of the mouth has the characteristic cottony appearance. And see how the sharp fangs are dripping with—"

At that moment, the snake's head whipped around toward me and, even though it should have been totally dead, tried to chomp down on my arm. Grandpa Sol turned and flung the head about thirty feet into the canal. Then he turned to me very calmly and said, "Oh, sometimes they do that."

So if you are still wondering why I am so naturally bad at staying out of trouble and danger, please consider that this man was my first babysitter. Honestly, it's amazing I've survived this long.

11. Sonnenblick-Ryan:
Battle of the Lightweights

If you think the news spreads fast when someone gets asked out, that is nothing compared to how fast the whole school finds out there's going to be a fight. When Jimmy and I walk out at the end of the day, we have a swarming tail of excited sixth graders spreading out behind us.

It's like watching sharks swarming after a bloody bucket of chum.

There are always tons of teachers outside at dismissal time. I don't know how none of them notice something is going on, but somehow we all troop past them around the corner of the school and half a block down, until Jimmy and I are at the far end of the high chain-link fence that surrounds the school's concrete playground. Then Jimmy stops walking. So do I. It feels weird and ceremonial. Geoff takes my glasses and my jean jacket. Mike takes Jimmy's jean jacket, but Jimmy keeps his glasses on. The crowd forms a wide half circle, trapping us between them and the fence.

It's pretty embarrassing and strange. I had a few fights in

elementary school, but none of them featured official corner-men or screaming fans. This is like some kind of crazy sporting event. Or a duel. Jimmy is one of the scrawniest people I have ever seen. What if he beats me up in front of all these people? I will have to transfer to Catholic school! I am sure the nuns will love me.

Yikes. I'd better not lose.

Jimmy and I circle around as the crowd starts chanting, "Fight! Fight! Fight!" You know, just in case Jimmy and I had been planning to engage in a bake-off or a rousing game of Go Fish instead.

It's really hard to throw the first punch, and I think Jimmy doesn't want to do it, either. But then someone pushes me from behind and I actually crash into Jimmy. He pushes me off. I push him back. It's on!

I have incredibly bad eyesight, so I figure my only chance is to make sure Jimmy stays close. It would also probably be a good idea to knock his glasses off. When Jimmy steps toward me again, I swing with a

long, sweeping right, which sends Jimmy's glasses flying into the mob.

Perfect!

Jimmy staggers backward, but as I step in, he gets in his first punch. His thumb jabs me in my left eye.

Not perfect! I was already blind enough, but now my eye is so full of stinging tears that I can't even really open it.

Also, I am mad. I shove Jimmy against the fence and start hitting him in the face and chest over and over. I am vaguely aware of Mike's voice shouting, "Hands up! Get your hands up!" to Jimmy. At the same time, Geoff is yelling, "Give him a knuckler in the schnoozer!" at the top of his lungs. Which I am sure would be very appro-priate if we were in a movie about 1920s gang-sters. Jimmy gets his fists up in front of his face, but I get in several more shots to his ribs before some-one pulls me away.

Suddenly, everybody is shouting, "Teachers! *Run!*"

Geoff hands me my glasses and my jacket and we take off down Castleton Avenue, away from the school. I am still blinking my left eye, but I don't think it is poked out or anything. I also notice that my hands and legs are shaking. I am out of breath, and my clothes are sweated through again.

The last thing I see before we duck down into a side street is Jimmy getting hustled away by Mike. Jimmy's face is red and blotchy. I wonder how he feels. He has lost. *In front of all those people.*

I have won, but I feel like crying. I really hope somebody saved Jimmy's glasses.

12. The Best Sleepovers Are the Ones Featuring Hazardous Trash Mounds

Even when things are going perfectly, I have trouble sleeping at night. My parents and Dr. Purow think it's because of my asthma medications. That might be part of it, but I also worry a lot, and the worries get much worse the instant the lights go off. When I was in elementary school, I even used to pull my hair out of my head in bed because I was so worried my mom would get in a car crash and die on her way home from her graduate-school classes in New Jersey. I've stopped pulling my hair out, but the worry is still there. I also worry a lot about my parents fighting. They fight about a lot of things, like which cars to buy, how much money to spend on stuff, and—especially—my mom's grad school. My dad thinks she should be home at night with my sister and me, but she thinks that is sexist and she should be allowed to work on her career. Sometimes I don't even know why they are fighting. And they aren't even consistent with it. There are short stretches when they get along fine. Then there are weeks when they snap at each other constantly. But the worst is when they don't talk to each other for days and days.

When they are in the middle of a not-talking streak, it makes me really mad. Tiptoeing around the house for a week because everybody is super tense just makes me want to break something. That is not a good sleeping mood.

Usually, I sleep much better when I am not home. Camp is great for sleeping, and so are other people's houses.

The night before my big date with Coty, I sleep at Geoff's house. I figure I need a good night's rest. But when we are lying in the dark in his double beds, I am shocked to find that I can't sleep. I just keep thinking of all the things that might go wrong at Skate Odyssey. What if my hair is sticking up and I don't know it? What if the rock band T-shirt I am planning to wear isn't fancy enough? What if I fall, break my arm, and have to be carted off in an ambulance while Coty tries hard not to laugh but fails?

And, of course, there's still the whole kissing thing hanging over me. I have only kissed a few girls in my life, and it was all just games and dares. I kissed three girls while playing spin the bottle at Camp Lenape two summers ago, and then there was that one time with Maria Popko from up the block when the older kids said we didn't have the guts to lock ourselves in my sister's room together.

Maria smelled like grape Dubble Bubble gum.

The problem is that none of those kisses gave me any info on whether I really know how to do this thing. I wish there had been scorecards, with a space at the bottom for constructive criticism: "Tilt your head to the side more!" "Ask before you kiss." "I recommend better dental hygiene." "Don't open your eyes, because that makes you look like a strange bottom-feeding fish from up close." You know, helpful stuff like that.

Also, I am not a traditionally handsome young man. Basically, on my good days I feel like a zit with glasses.

I sit up and ask Geoff about his first date with his supermodel-like girlfriend, Jennifer Jones. He tells me I will know what to do if I just "relax and let things happen."

This is the dumbest thing I've ever heard in my life. When fighter pilots show up for their first day of basic training, does the instructor just hand them the keys to their jets and say, "Here you go. Take 'er up! Just relax and let things happen!"? I don't think so. Going out with girls is an extremely complicated subject, requiring tons of knowledge and thousands of hours of practice. The problem is that Geoff is so smooth and slick at this stuff because he has been good with girls since forever. He doesn't even know how much he knows.

I sit there for so long, sighing, that eventually Geoff reaches out and turns on the lamp between our beds. "What's wrong?" he asks.

I crack completely, and my darkest fear slips out of my mouth before I can stop it. "Geoff, am I the ugliest kid in the world?"

He swings his legs over the edge of his bed, sits up, and looks me up and down for a long time. Finally, he says, "I've seen worse." Then he clicks his lamp back off, and a few minutes later, his breathing slows down so I know he is asleep.

I lie there for what feels like a thousand years, staring up at the dark blur of Geoff's ceiling and thinking, *I've seen worse? What does* that *mean?*

Geoff's house has a breezeway connecting the living room to the garage. This is like a screened-in path with a roof. The breezeway is getting torn down and replaced with a real room, so there is a giant pile of construction debris pushed up at the curb behind Geoff's garbage cans. It's all in huge black garbage bags, but you can tell by the bulges in the bags that whatever's inside is jagged and pointy.

Naturally, the only thing for us to do when we wake up in the morning is to use this Mound of Peril for an epic bike stunt. Our newest trick is the intentional crash, which is perfect for the situation. Even though it is surprisingly hot out for a fall morning, we both put on our denim jackets for protection. Then we line up our bikes in the middle of Geoff's street, about thirty feet from the two garbage cans.

The goal is to build up enough speed and momentum to send us flying up and over our handlebars, ideally in a somersault so that we land on our backs on top of the trash bags. If we go too slowly, we won't get in a full midair rotation, and landing face-first seems like a bad plan. The other key to this whole thing is that we have to aim our front tires perfectly so they get crammed between the two trash cans. This will stop the bikes sharply and give us maximum lift during the critical ejection phase.

Geoff goes first. He does a total Evel Knievel. His front wheel is slightly crooked at the moment of impact, so he is flung slightly sideways. This means he does a half twist in the air and tumbles upon impact, bouncing off the trash pile and landing on the lawn. I go charging over to see whether he is alive, but before I even jump off my bike, he is sitting up on the grass, laughing his head off.

It seems that "relax and let things happen" actually works as stuntman advice.

We spend so long crashing into the pile again and again that the sun is straight overhead when we are done, and we are forced to stop because the black garbage bags have gotten too hot to touch. Also, some of the bags have ripped open, revealing that they are filled with some surprising items, like bent nails, broken glass, and bits of the workmen's food leftovers.

Geoff and I have avoided getting any alarming gashes or punctures, but as we enter the house to eat lunch, his mom gives us a dirty look.

"What, Mom?" Geoff asks.

"You both stink! What were you doing out there, rolling through a dumpster?"

I have to say, she's pretty close.

When I get home, I jump right in the shower. After a morning of tumbling over trash and landing on grass (which is a deathly allergy of mine), it feels incredibly great to lather up all over with soap and shampoo. (Well, except when the soap hits my face and I realize I am kind of scratched up from the morning's daredevil activities.)

I am going to smell great on this date! I think.

But when I wash everything off, I am horrified to note that I still reek. In fact, it takes five cycles of lather, rinse, and repeat before I smell like a human being again.

Hopefully.

13. A Note Regarding My History with Inhalers

One thing I should probably mention before we go any further is that my mom is kind of overprotective. She makes me wear a seat belt in the car! She didn't let me ride my bike in the street until I was nearly six years old! She constantly bugs me to make sure I have a spare pair of glasses whenever I am going to sleep at someone's house. She's even trying to make me bring an incredibly dorky pair of prescription goggles to camp next summer for waterskiing—just because I crashed into a wooden float *one* time last year.

So you can just imagine how much she worries about my asthma. I admit, I have had some problems in the past with inhalers. Specifically, I often forget to carry one, and if I am carrying one, I sometimes lose it. My mom thinks I forget them on purpose because I don't like the way the medicine makes me feel.

That is totally unfair and untrue. I forget them on purpose because having to carry an inhaler everywhere is embarrassing.

Anyway, my mom is obsessed with making sure I always

have an inhaler. She nags me every time I leave the house: "Do you have an inhaler?" In fact, she usually nags me over and over again. But in case that doesn't work, she also activates her backup plan. She sticks the inhalers in my backpack without telling me. She puts two of them in my camp trunk AND mails one directly to the camp nurse. She gives one to my grandparents if I am going to sleep in their condominium. Honestly, she would probably staple one to my face if she could, just to be sure it was *right there*.

And okay, the condominium thing kind of makes sense because of that one time I was chasing a lizard up a tree by the pool and stepped barefoot on a mound of fire ants. My sister ran to get my Grandma Lillian, who made me do two puffs on the way to the emergency room. As my feet swelled up to roughly the size of regulation NFL footballs, my heart started pounding about a million times a minute and I thought I was going to faint. But at least I didn't die from wheezing.

On the other hand, they gave me a massive shot of adrenaline at the hospital, along with enough Benadryl to knock out a racehorse, so I would probably have survived anyway.

Since then, my mom has been even more dedicated to stashing inhalers everywhere. Which doesn't really make sense, because if I am actually having a deadly asthma attack and don't have an inhaler in my pocket, how am I supposed to know where to find the hidden inhaler that might be around? I mean, she is pretty creative. I have found inhalers in the middle of a folded towel, zipped into the hood compartment of my ski jacket, and, on one very memorable occasion, in the Yankees bag I always took to my Little League games. Unfortunately, I didn't discover that one until I threw the bag across the dugout and a kid dropped an aluminum bat on it.

As it turns out, the metal canister part of an inhaler is pretty strong, but the plastic mist-shooter part shatters pretty easily.

The worst inhaler incident, by far, happened when I slept over at Craig Easton's house last spring. I hadn't seen Craig since camp the summer before, so we were both pretty excited. We immediately decided to have a pillow fight, just like the legendary ones we always used to have in our cabin. As I was putting on my pj's and getting ready, Craig whacked me over the head from behind with his pillow. So I grabbed my own pillow and swung it right at his head.

CRACK! Craig fell down on the bed holding his nose, which was spouting a pretty impressive amount of blood. "What the heck, Jordan?" Craig asked.

Well, he didn't actually say *heck*.

I was stunned for a second. I just kept thinking, *Pillows don't go CRACK!* Then it occurred to me to check inside my pillowcase. I reached in there, and my hand closed around the cold metal of—you guessed it!—an inhaler. By this time, Craig's mom had charged into the room to see what was going on. As soon as she saw me standing over her bleeding child with a metal object in my hand, she started to scream.

I tried to explain, but nothing worked. My mom had to drive all the way back to the south shore of the island to get me, and I left Craig's house in disgrace. I haven't heard from him yet this fall, and I am not exactly holding my breath.

I hope I grow out of this asthma thing before I die from it. Or, more likely, before I accidentally kill someone else.

14. Love and Death at Skate Odyssey

After I am done with the longest shower in history, I look through the medicine cabinet for my dad's aftershave. I have watched him put on this stuff a thousand times: He applies just a little bit onto each of his hands, and then kind of slaps it onto both of his cheeks at once. This doesn't look like some complicated brain-genius operation, at least until I attempt it for myself.

The problem is the "just a little bit" part. You have to turn the bottle upside down in order to pour the aftershave onto your hands, and the stuff is a liquid. As anyone who has ever seen my handwriting can tell you, I am not exactly known for my fine motor coordination.

My first attempt does not go well, at least if the goal is not to splash a quarter of the bottle onto the counter and down the sink drain. On my second attempt, I am so afraid to spill more of the stuff that I barely get any onto my hands at all. When I slap it on, I don't think I smell any different.

It is kind of hard to tell when I am standing over a vanity that has just been drenched in so much aftershave that if I light a match, it would probably blow up the entire house.

Possibly the block.

But I definitely don't want to go too light on the romantic scent, especially when I am a bit worried about the possibility of sweating all over the place, and have also been rolling on a trash pile for several hours. I go for a third splash. This time, I don't spill anything, and both of my palms are glistening, so I figure I have done this thing right. I slap both of my cheeks. Then I whimper.

It turns out that aftershave is mostly alcohol. And of course, my face is mostly a network of open scratches. What a refreshing combination!

By the time I am dressed in my best Led Zeppelin shirt, faded jeans, my cool special-occasion jean jacket with the Beatles, Led Zeppelin, and AC/DC patches, and a pair of fashionably worn-in Puma Clyde sneakers, the sting in my face is mostly gone. I head downstairs to tell my mom it's time to go. She smiles at me at first, but then she wrinkles her nose.

"Did you put on—*aftershave?*" she asks.

I can feel myself blushing. "Yeah," I say. "So?"

"Oh, honey," she says, smiling. "You're not supposed to use the whole bottle."

I don't know what to do. Should I rush up and take another shower? Try to scrub my face in the sink without soaking my best shirt? Postpone the date until I no longer smell like a cross between a perfume factory and the landfill?

My mom rubs my hair. "It's okay," she says. "We'll just keep the car windows rolled down. By the way, do you have your inhaler?"

When we pull up to the curb in front of Coty's house, my mom beeps the horn *three times*. "Mom!" I say. "What are you doing?"

"I'm using a device called the *car horn*. It is used to catch the attention of people who are outside the car."

"You're hilarious," I mutter. "But couldn't you just beep once?"

She moves her hand like she is going to beep again.

"Ha ha," I say. "Please be cool. Please?"

"That's me, Jord. Your cool mom. Coolest mother in town."

"Shh!" I hiss. "She's coming out!"

I jump out of the car and hurry up the long front walk of Coty's house so we can have a tiny bit of privacy before my mom gets a chance to talk to Coty. But when we meet in the middle of the walk, I can't think of anything to say. She is basically wearing the same stuff she wears every day: a Styx T-shirt, her jean jacket with the big Harley-Davidson patch across the shoulders, and tight jeans with a belt made from the chain of a motorcycle. But she looks different, older. I think she is wearing makeup, because when she blinks, I see that her eyelids are blue. My hands start to sweat. After a few agonizing moments of staring at her, I say, "Uh, hi, Coty!"

This is probably a good start, because it establishes that I know her name. Also, that I am friendly.

Coty stares back. "Uh, hi, Jordan."

Whew, I think. *She remembers my name, too.*

I try to think of what Geoff would say. "Hey," I cough out, feeling myself blushing again. "You look nice."

Eek, did that sound creepy? Is she going to turn around, go back into her house, and dead bolt the door?

Finally, she smiles. She really does look nice today. "You, too," she says. We stare at each other some more, until I am almost hoping my mom will honk the horn again just to break up the awkward scene.

"Um, we should probably go," I say. Coty nods, and we head back to the car, walking stiffly side by side, not making eye contact, like a pair of rock-and-roll robots. *Why is this so hard?* I wonder. Usually, we never run out of stuff to talk about, even on the phone. But this is different.

This is a DATE. A DATE with a real live girl. A real live girl I like. And we are going to be alone together for two whole hours!

This situation is kind of a nightmare, if you think about it.

I hold the car door open for Coty, which I think is pretty smooth. As I am closing it, I catch a glimpse of my mom grinning in the front seat. I go around the back of the car and sit behind my mom, who pulls the car away from the curb without saying anything. Then Coty says, "Hi, Mrs. Sonnenblick."

My mom says, "Hello, Coty. It's so nice to finally meet you. Jordan talks about you all the time!" I can hear from her voice that she is still smiling. This is probably the most fun thing that has ever happened to her. Ugh. Some coolest mom.

"He does?" Coty asks.

If this car had an ejection seat, I'd be pressing the button on mine right about now. Or possibly on my mom's.

"Mom," I say, jumping in before she can start telling stories from my childhood or something equally horrifying, "can you please turn the radio on?"

She gives me a look in the rearview mirror, but she hits the power button on the radio. An awesome, brand-new song is playing: "The Tide Is High," by Blondie. Coty starts playing the beat on her lap at the exact time I start playing it on mine. Then she sneaks her left hand across the space between us and hits my leg, and we both laugh. Our heads come together in the middle of the back seat and I catch a whiff of perfume.

Excellent! Now she won't be able to tell if I smell too sweaty, aftershave-y, or garbage-y.

Maybe this whole date thing might have a slight chance of being all right.

When we arrive at Skate Odyssey, my mom says, "Jord, did you remember to bring snack money?"

Snack money? Really, Mom? Am I supposed to be buying Coty some apple juice and a box of animal crackers? We're not five. Sheesh.

"I have money," I say.

"And are you sure you have your—"

I cut her off again. She is about to say *inhaler*—possibly the least romantic word in the English language. "Yes, Mom. I have everything I need." Actually, I am not 100 percent sure I have my inhaler, but then I pat the left waist-level pocket of my jean jacket as we are getting out of the car, and it's definitely there. Whew. Between the perfume and the aftershave, plus the smell of moldy rental skates and the stress of this whole boy-girl thing, I figure there's about a fifty-fifty chance I'll start wheezing any minute.

It's a little awkward when I pay for Coty's ticket and her skate rental, but also a little cool. Then we are out on the hardwood floor of the rink. A disco ball is spinning, and laser lights are bouncing off it in all directions. I spend the first two songs trying to get up the courage to hold Coty's hand. I feel like I have to grab her hand soon, before the lights get super dim and the music slows down for the Couples' Skate. If we aren't holding hands when the Couples' Skate starts, then we'll have to go through a whole weird *Do you want to stay on for the Couples' Skate or should we get off and buy a snack?* conversation.

There's that word again: *snack*. If I could get through the date without sounding like a kindergartener, that would be kind of nice.

I am saved by accident. An older teenage guy zooms past me, skating backward, showing off, and smashes right into the backs of three girls who are immediately in front of us. The girls kind of fly up in the air and land right on top of the dude, like it's a cartoon or something.

This makes us have to swerve really hard to avoid the pileup and then bounce off a wall. It also makes us crack up laughing. Somehow, Coty and I grab on to each other for balance. I get a fistful of her jean jacket, and she slings her arm all the way around my waist from behind. Once we are past the scene of the mini tragedy, everything suddenly feels very serious. I look over at Coty, and her eyes are partly covered by her hair. She has this habit of blowing up on her bangs when this happens, and suddenly, we are staring right at each other from just a few inches away. She lets go of my waist and grabs my hand.

Well, I think, *that was easy.*

Then somebody taps me on the shoulder. It's the older kid who caused the big pileup. I have a moment of panic. Is he mad at me? Did I step on him as we were swerving? Is he going to beat me up in front of my date? Because that would be embarrassing.

"Hey," he says, holding one hand out next to me. "I think you dropped this!" He's holding my inhaler. I grab it, mumble a very quiet thank-you, and shove it deep in my pocket.

That might have been more embarrassing than getting beaten up, I think. *There's nothing worse than a Good Samaritan.*

But Coty doesn't let go of my hand, or giggle, or anything. So I guess it is kind of okay.

We stay on for the Couples' Skate. It's three terrible, slow, mushy pop songs in a row. Don't tell anybody, but for the first time in my life, I am enjoying REO Speedwagon. No, more than that, I am *grooving* to REO Speedwagon.

As the lights come back up, we get off the rink and buy drinks. I am a little afraid that Dr Pepper might cause bad breath, so when Coty goes to the bathroom, I rush back to the counter and buy a pack of the only gum they have, which is Fruit Stripe. It's not mint, but I hope it's better than nothing. When Coty gets back, I suavely offer her the first piece from the pack. I take the second.

I am not sure exactly what to do now. I am pretty sure there is supposed to be kissing. I see a dark little elevated seating area that looks over one corner of the rink. There's nobody up there. I can feel my voice shaking as I ask, "Um, do you want to watch the skaters for a while?"

How dumb am I? *Watch the skaters?* Are they doing tricks out there? Is this the roller-skating Olympic trials?

"Sure," Coty says, grabbing my hand again as we stand up.

How smart am I? *Watch the skaters!* So simple, yet so bold!

The only problem with my genius plan is that now we actually have to go up there and stand like idiots watching the skaters. And I am sure she knows I am just taking her into this shadowy corner to kiss her. She gives me that sly Coty grin, and I know she knows *I know* she knows I am just taking her into this corner to kiss her.

I probably wait too long to make my move. I keep telling myself to wait for a romantic song, but nothing romantic comes on. First, it's "Saturday Night," an ancient song by the Bay City Rollers—pretty uncool as a soundtrack for my first real kiss. I get my hopes up for the next song, but it turns out to be "Play That Funky Music," which I admit is funky. It's still not romantic, though.

I am pretty sure I hear Coty sigh as the funky music fades out, so I vow that no matter what the next song is, I am going to go for it. As a fast bass-and-drums groove comes booming out of the speaker five feet away, I nearly groan. It's "Another One Bites the Dust."

Which, again, is pretty funky. It is also literally about death. On the other hand, Coty isn't going to wait around for too many more songs, and my Fruit Stripe is losing flavor by the minute. I turn to her, take her other hand, and look her straight in the eyes.

Remember that dumb thing I said earlier about how Coty wasn't beautiful like some of the other girls in my class? At that moment, I realize I was strangely right. She's not beautiful like anybody else: She's beautiful like *Coty*.

It's a bit tricky on skates, but we kind of pull together and our lips meet. Not exactly gently, but the maneuver isn't a total disaster. The whole thing only lasts maybe two seconds, but hey—it happens, and Coty doesn't push me away. Or slap me. Or, worst of all, *laugh*.

"So, uh, I guess we should skate some more," I stammer.

"That's a solid plan," Coty says. "This being a skating rink and all."

Well, now she *is* laughing at me. But I'm laughing with her.

Before I know it, the lights all over the rink turn all the way on, so bright it makes both of us squint for a moment. Holy cow! It's almost five o'clock! I promised my mom we would be waiting outside at five sharp. And I have a terrifying hunch that if we are not out there on time, my mom might *come in*.

As we sit down on one of the benches and start taking off our skates, "We Are the Champions" comes on.

Yeah, we are, I think.

15. When Falling Off the Roof Is the Good News

Usually, falling off the roof of a house would be the worst event of your week. The week after my big date, I fall off the roof of my house. The good news is that I survive. The bad news is that the fall isn't even one of the *top four* worst events of my week.

The problems start on Monday in English class. Miss Sarisky hands out the novel we are supposed to be reading in class for the next million weeks: *Great Expectations* by Charles Dickens. First of all, it looks super boring. I love reading, but usually when I am choosing something to read, it has to pass four tests:

- Does this book contain magic?
- Does this book contain explosions?
- Does this book feature athletic feats and/or other heroic acts of derring-do?
- Is this book very, very old?

The correct answers are YES, YES, YES, and HECK, NO!

From Miss Sarisky's description and the writing on the back cover, the score for *Great Expectations* is a disgusting NO, NO, NO, YES.

But that isn't the terrible part. The terrible part, which we discover as she thunks down hardcover copies on the first desk in each row and the kids start passing them back, is that these books smell incredibly awful—like they have been stored for thirty years in the corner of a public bathroom. Kids all over the room are making faces, waving their hands to clear the air, and even beginning to sneeze and cough.

"This book weighs like nine pounds!" Shoshana exclaims.

"And it's *five hundred and forty-four pages* long!" Elizabeth Maersh gasps.

"And the paper is all yellow!" Joshua adds.

Then Geoff shouts out, "These books smell BARFY!"

He is not wrong.

Everybody is looking around in a panic. We can't spend the next marking period carrying around these horrible, contaminated copies of a long, boring book we don't want to read in the first place. When my copy hits my desk, I pick it up, and as the smell wafts over me, I notice that there are visible black dots of mold all over the edges of the pages.

I refuse to die of asthma because of Miss Sarisky. I slam the book down. "NO BARFY BOOKS!" I yell.

"NO BARFY BOOKS!" people around the room chant. "NO BARFY BOOKS! NO BARFY BOOKS!" In a flash, everybody starts passing the books back up to the front of the room.

It seems I have learned nothing from last year's library-squad strike, because here I am again, leading a rebellion.

Miss Sarisky makes a big show of straightening out the pile of books on the front desk of each row. "We'll just leave these here," she hisses. "For NOW!" From the snarl on her face, I get the feeling she's even less pleased with me than Mrs. Rainbow was.

But that's only the first disaster of the week. The second one happens in math class. Usually, when we walk in, Mrs. Lee is writing a warm-up problem on the board, which is an awesome sight to see, because she has the amazing ability to write with both hands at once. Once, she even wrote with both hands while counting aloud—in Chinese! She is probably too talented to be a teacher. I hope she doesn't leave to join the circus.

Anyway, on this day there's no warm-up problem. Mrs. Lee says, "Today we're going to be doing something different. Something fun!"

I already know this is going to be bad. Last year, my math teacher assigned us the "fun" project of making a poster-sized calendar of a whole month using Roman numerals for the dates. I loved my math teacher, so I spent the entire weekend making a spectacularly artistic, mathematically correct poster. When she handed back everybody's project a week later, she singled out a few of the best ones. I was waiting on the edge of my seat, sure that my poster was going to be among them, but it wasn't. Then she handed back every single kid's poster except mine and dismissed the rest of the class to recess. I went up to her and asked where my poster was.

"Jordan," she said, "your poster was lovely! It was bright! It was colorful! It was the wrong month!"

So when Mrs. Lee starts talking about *math* and *fun* in the same sentence, I start to sweat. It turns out there's a city-wide contest. Six times, spread throughout the year, every middle school kid in New York is going to do a set of six word problems. There will be a big award ceremony at City Hall with the mayor for the kids who get a perfect 36 out of 36 at the end.

I keep waiting for the "fun" part.

This is the exact kind of trap I spend my life trying to avoid. The teacher will urge me to get all the problems right, as though that is a good thing. But the kids will hate me if I am the only one in the class to get all the problems right. I resolve then and there to purposely get a problem wrong.

But the problems are so easy for me that I zip through the whole set. In fact, Mrs. Lee asks me three times if I want to check my work, because I am the first one done. But there's no point—the answers all popped into my head right away, and for me, the first answer is always the best answer.

Sure enough, I am the only kid in the class who gets them all right. Worse than that, I am the only kid in the grade who gets them all right. Several of the seventh and eighth graders on the math team get all six. Peter Friedman is one of them. He tells me after school that the math team coach wants to invite me to join the team.

The next day, Mr. Overbye stops me in the hallway to congratulate me and strongly urges me to stop by with him to say hi to the math team coach. I tell him I am late for band, but I promise I will "look into it." I have learned this trick from my parents. When I want something and they don't want to come right out and say no, they say, "We'll look into it."

This is awful! Math is easy for me, but I hate it. Being on the math team is my worst nightmare. That's like wearing a bright orange T-shirt with I'M SMART AND I LIKE TO SHOW OFF on the front. Also, it involves doing extra math.

No, thank you.

Next time, I have to get a problem wrong before this whole thing gets even more out of hand.

The third disaster hits me that night, and it is mostly my fault. My grandparents call from Florida, and I am the one closest to the phone on the wall of the kitchen. My grandmother spends about half an hour talking about how the grandson of her friends, the Gillarys, just had the loveliest bar mitzvah— at least as nice as the one her other friends, the Pomerantzes, had the week before.

"Such nice boys," she says. "Jacob Gillary looked so

handsome in his suit, and he even called his grandparents up to say a blessing on the bread at the party. Sylvia looked so thrilled. I can *only imagine* the pride she must have felt." Then she doesn't say anything for twenty seconds or so. I feel like I am drowning in the silence.

And the guilt. My grandmother's biggest regret is that my mom doesn't belong to a temple, which means there is no big, blowout bar mitzvah in my seventh-grade future. My mom is an only child, and my sister had zero interest in having a bat mitzvah, so I am Grandma's last chance. I know she is probably thinking about how disgraced she will be in front of all the ladies at her Jewish women's group in Florida when I visit next year and she has to tell everyone I'm not coming through for her in the clutch.

And Grandma is the president of the entire Tamarac, Florida, chapter. What an embarrassment! What a disgrace! What a *shanda*, as we say in Yiddish. Well, I don't say it in Yiddish, because I have no Jewish education.

This is not an entirely fair situation. Grandma is the one who married a guy whose favorite story is how he jumped out the window to flee a rabbi at age five. That might have been a clue to her about how the kid and the grandkids would turn out.

But she's not giving Grandpa Sol the dreaded Twenty Seconds of Guilt. She's not giving my mom the dreaded Twenty Seconds of Guilt. She isn't even splitting the time up, so that each of us gets Six Point Six-Seven Seconds of Guilt.

Nope, all that guilt is raining down upon me like some kind of biblical plague.

Not that I know anything about those, with my miserable lack of Hebrew schooling.

Here's the part that *is* my fault: I crack. Lissa never cracks when my grandmother starts slinging the guilt around. When my grandmother says, "Lissa, someone should really match up all these socks and fold them neatly," Lissa just says, "You're right, Grandma, someone totally should."

But I am not Lissa. "Grandma," I say, "I've been thinking. Would you like it if *I* had a bar mitzvah?"

Why did I say *I've been thinking*? Clearly, I have *not* been thinking about this at all. I fell asleep during Peter Friedman's brother's bar mitzvah last year. I don't know how to read Hebrew. And oh, yeah, my parents are not members of a temple, which means there's no way I can just snap my fingers and make a bar mitzvah happen. What am I supposed to do now—dial 1-800-RENT-A-RABBI?

"Oh, sweetheart, I would love that. But are you sure it's what *you* want?"

Okay, I think, *here's your out. She handed it to you. Now take it!*

"Yes, Grandma. I want to make you proud."

My parents are staring at me in horror. My sister is staring at me in horror. I wish we had a mirror in the kitchen so *I* could be staring at me in horror. I can't believe this! Now I have a little more than a year to learn a whole new language, a bunch of baffling rituals, and six thousand years of history.

This is seriously going to cut into my Atari time. If I never get to the eleventh level of *Space Invaders*, it's totally Grandma's fault.

On Wednesday, the whole roof-falling thing happens. It's one of the days I take the city bus to the corner of Victory Boulevard and Highland Avenue, then walk down a few houses, cut through a backyard, and jump over a fence to get home. When I walk around the side of my house to the front door and reach in my jacket pocket, I find an inhaler, but not my keys. I reach into the hidden inside pocket of my backpack and find yet another inhaler, but still no keys. At first, I think, *No problem. I'll just use the key we keep under the rock in the bushes.* When I flip the rock over, I don't find the spare key *or* an inhaler, though I do find a whole lot of centipedes and a pretty cool red-backed salamander.

My mom is going to be at her office at the College of Staten Island for another couple of hours. My sister has chorus practice. And my dad never gets home from his job as a doctor until everyone else has already been home for a while.

I am going to be locked out for hours. The good news is that it's a warm day, so I probably won't freeze to death during my ordeal. I also won't suffocate, because I have two brand-new inhalers on me. That's like 288 puffs' worth. The bad news is that I know my mom is going to call the house in twenty minutes to make sure I got home alive, and she is going to freak when I don't answer. Also, I am bored!

After carefully considering these pros and cons, I decide I have no other choice but to break into my house. Fortunately, Lissa has left the window of her bedroom, which is above our front porch, partly open. She always does that, even though it drives my parents crazy and they constantly bug her to close it, because *Lissa doesn't crack*. She does whatever she wants. At home, I am the goody-goody. I know this because she calls me one on a daily basis.

Well, now being good requires being bad.

I look around to make sure none of the neighbors are watching. Clearly, getting arrested for breaking into my own home would make a bad problem worse. Nobody, not even nosy old Carmella from up the street, is looking, so I slip into the two-foot-wide alley that separates my house from Eric Warheit's. I put my back against my house and my feet against Eric's, and start kind of squirm-crawling my way up to the roof. This is pretty exhausting. You have to push your butt up as far as it will go by straightening your legs. Then you have to bend your legs one at a time until they are crunched up almost to your chest, and straighten them again so that your butt goes a couple of feet higher. Once you have done this eight or nine times, you are there!

Well, except for the skin of your lower back, which is mostly scraped off against the wall of your house.

When I get up to the edge of our roof, I experience the terrifying moment when, in order to get out of the alley and onto the surface of the roof, I have to do a challenging half-twist, half-push-up maneuver. Falling between the houses would be bad. Both walls are made of really rough stucco—good for climbing, but not so good for tumbling down. And the floor of the alley is concrete.

When I flip onto the extremely steep roof, I lie on my stomach for a moment and catch my breath. Then I peek across the street. Still no Carmella, thankfully. I sit up so my feet are facing the edge of the roof, my butt is straight uphill from my feet, and my hands are braced against the shingles on either side of me.

Our roof has two levels. I am on top of the garage, which is the lower level. Lissa's window is about twelve feet to my right and three feet above me, on the higher level. I crab-walk sideways until I get to the edge of the upper roof. Here's another really scary part: I have to stand up and then use my hands to push my body up onto the next level. I nearly have a heart attack when one of my sneakers starts to skid down the shingles, but I catch myself in time.

I am not sure Puma basketball shoes are recommended for rooftop use.

Anyway, once I am on the top roof, I just have to get on my butt again and push myself up a few feet to reach Lissa's open window. Our house is something called a Cape Cod, which means Lissa's window is something called a "dormer." It sticks up and out of the surface of the regular roof, and then has its own little mini roof on top. This is kind of good, because if we just had a straight two-story house, I wouldn't be able to break in this way.

What am I talking about? I am still not able to break in this way, because while Lissa has left her window open, she has thoughtfully closed and locked her window screen so that no bugs, squirrels, or innocent little brothers can get into the house. With my back pressed up next to the open window, I try hard to pop the screen out of its frame. But the problem is that the harder I push the screen in, the harder I am pushing myself *off the roof.*

What would Evel Knievel do? I ask myself. The answer is obvious: He would push even harder.

Stupid Evel Knievel. I give one last mighty, awkward back-handed heave against the screen, which succeeds in popping open one corner. It also succeeds in making my other hand and both of my feet lose their grip on the roof. I slide down several feet to the very edge, but then my left heel gets jammed into the rain gutter.

I am saved!

For about four seconds, until the gutter breaks off.

16. Sonnenblick-Thompson: The Revenge Match

It turns out falling off the roof of your house isn't such a big deal as long as you manage to land on a nice soft bush. Well, it's not a big deal for you. It's pretty catastrophic for the bush, though. Between that and the broken rain gutter, I have some explaining to do when my mom's car comes screeching into the driveway twenty minutes later.

"Why in the world would you climb onto the roof?" my mom asks me.

"I climbed onto the roof because I didn't want you to worry," I reply.

In my defense, this had sounded much better in my head.

At dinner, I get yelled at again by my mom. I get yelled at by my dad. I get a hearty low five from Lissa under the table. "Not bad, nerd-bomber," she whispers to me when our parents are distracted. I'm pretty sure that is the nicest thing she has said to me since she hit the troubled teen years.

At least I get a good story out of it. But as I am telling my epic tale to Joshua Stern and James Padilla in homeroom the next day, I am interrupted by Jimmy Ryan.

"I'm glad you didn't die, Jordan," he says.

I am stunned by Jimmy's thoughtfulness. Who knew he was so gracious, so bighearted, so generous of spirit, so—

"Because now my cousin Michael will get a chance to pound you to a pulp! Friday, after school. Playground."

"Wait!" Joshua says. *Thank you, Joshua!* I think. *I don't have anything against Michael. Also, he is huge. Someone needs to stop this madness.*

"What?" Jimmy snaps.

"Do you mean Friday as in tomorrow? Or do you mean, like, *next* Friday?"

"Tomorrow," Jimmy says.

"Oh, okay," Joshua replies.

I have no idea why I have to fight Michael. In elementary school, winning a fistfight meant that, at worst, you'd have to face a rematch with *that same kid.* Apparently, in middle school, it just means you've won the level, like in a video game. I guess Cousin Michael is Level Two.

What's Level Three—Jimmy's mom? A tag-team match against a couple of aunts?

Michael is built like a cross between a regular sixth grader and a bulldozer. He is going to pummel me. But at the end of the next school day, feeling the swelling wave of kids behind us, propelling us out of the school and along the playground fence, I know that getting a couple of black eyes from Michael is a small price to pay compared to having everybody know I'm a chicken.

We don't even get all the way to the end of the fence before a full circle forms around us and stops us from going any farther. This time, I keep my glasses. Michael doesn't wear any, so I feel like I need to be able to see at the start of the battle.

Michael says to me, quietly, "You know, you can still stop this. Just tell Jimmy you're sorry. He's right there." Which is true. Jimmy is five feet away, holding Michael's backpack.

But everybody in the grade is watching. Geoff is there. Dougie is there. Joshua and James Padilla are there. And don't even get me started on the girls. It's either get creamed in this fight or wear a bag over my head for the next three years.

Oh well, I think. *Might as well get this over with.*

"What are you, afraid?" I ask.

Mike responds by punching me in the jaw, so fast I can't even step backward to reduce the impact. My head snaps back on my neck like I just got hit with a sledgehammer. I taste blood on my top lip, which has split open against my front teeth. But I don't reach up to rub it. Rubbing it makes you look weak.

I rear back and punch Michael right on the tip of his chin. Then we both stand and stare each other down. I don't want to get punched again, and I have a weird feeling Michael doesn't want to punch me again, but the crowd is screaming. I don't know how either of us can stop this thing. It hasn't even been a real fight so far—more like a Mutually Agreed-Upon Exchange of Punches.

Our fans seem to expect more.

Then, suddenly, I feel a hand grabbing a fistful of my jean-jacket collar. At the same time, another hand shoots out over my shoulder and grabs the front of Michael's T-shirt. The rest of the kids all run away as Michael and I are dragged up against the fence. I twist my neck, which feels sore, and see that both of us are in the iron grip of an old lady. She has bright red hair, and is somehow managing to clamp a huge umbrella under the arm that is also holding Michael. It's not raining, but with that thing, she is prepared for a hurricane.

"I'm a teacher at this school," she says, leaning the umbrella against the fence and taking out a pen and a notepad from her purse. "I am going to write down your names and phone numbers so I can call your parents this weekend. And *then* I'll see you on Monday!" I look at Michael, thinking maybe we can make a run for it. I am pleased to see that I have caught him rubbing his chin, until I realize I am rubbing my lip.

We exchange embarrassed smiles and give her our phone numbers.

You can imagine what my weekend is like. I try to make sure that, whatever I am doing, I am close enough to a telephone so that I can lunge and grab it before anybody else if a call comes in. It's hard to look casual while leaning against the kitchen wall reading comic books for half an hour at a time, or perching on the desk in my father's home office while he leans back in his reclining chair watching a baseball game on

TV. "Why don't you relax?" my parents say to me fifteen times over the course of the weekend.

I don't have an answer. I feel like I am waiting to be called in front of a firing squad. Geoff invites me to go roller-skating on Friday night and I say no, because if the phone call comes while I am out of the house, my parents will come and yank me off the rink in disgrace. On Saturday, I spend the entire day inside, constantly prepared to pounce on the phone if it rings. On Sunday morning, my dad tells me he's going out to the store to buy the newspaper. I am supposed to come. We have done this every week since I was a little kid. He gets the paper, Lissa gets candy, and I get three comic books.

I am dying to buy the new issue of *Uncanny X-Men*. This month, they're facing "THE SAVAGE FURY OF WEN-DI-GO!" Which sounds pretty awesome. But my mom never comes along, which means I have to skip this week. When the choice is *X-Men #140* or my life, I have to go with the life option.

When my dad and Lissa get back, she happily waves a bag of Twizzlers in my face. "You really should have come, Jord," she says. And she's right, because the phone was silent the whole time they were out.

By the end of the afternoon, I am in such a panic that I can't take it anymore. I sneak into my dad's office, grab the telephone book, and risk taking it upstairs to my room to look up Michael's number. I can't stand the lack of information. I need to know whether the old teacher lady has called his parents.

Calling Michael is clearly the move of a desperate man. But ironically, Michael is now my only ally.

Unfortunately, there are a lot of Thompsons in the phone book.

I mean, a *lot* of Thompsons.

But at the eleventh number I try, when I ask to speak with Michael, the woman who answers the phone says, "Sure, honey. Hold on a second."

Weird! That sounded like it was probably Michael's mom. I punched her kid in the face and then she called me "honey."

Unfortunately, when Michael gets on the phone, I find out pretty quickly that he is a six-year-old who goes to P.S. 35, my old elementary school. I wish him a happy first-grade year and hang up.

Apparently, there are even a lot of *Michael* Thompsons on Staten Island.

On the fourteenth try, I hit the jackpot. After only half a ring, someone picks up the phone with a clatter, like they've knocked it off the wall.

The voice of an out-of-breath kid says, "Hello?"

"Hi," I say. "I'm calling for Michael Thompson. I'm in his class at school, and—"

"Jordan?" the kid asks. Finally, I've found the *right* Michael.

"Um, yeah."

"Did the red-haired umbrella lady call?" he whispers urgently.

"No. Did she call you?"

"No! What is wrong with this woman?" Michael asks. "Does she *enjoy* torturing kids and ruining their weekend?"

"I know, right? I haven't left my house since I got home on Friday. I'm afraid to leave the kitchen and miss her call."

"Dude," Michael says, "I'm afraid to pee! I wish somebody would invent some kind of *portable phone* or something so I could bring it to the bathroom!"

I laugh. Michael is having the same exact weekend I am. Also, he's funny. A portable phone? Genius.

We talk for like twenty minutes. When I hang up, I can't believe it. Somehow, we have become almost friends.

Almost.

17. WEEK OF THE PHANTOM TEACHER

Michael and I spend the whole next week waiting to hear from the lady. Every time the intercom crackles, we exchange looks of terror. Same thing if somebody knocks on our classroom door. And when Mr. Overbye strides into Miss Sarisky's class on Wednesday, I feel total, full-body panic. When I glance across the room at Michael, he looks like he might wet himself.

But The Bee isn't here to yell at Michael and me. Well, he is, but he's here to yell at everybody else, too. Miss Sarisky stands right next to him and smirks as his voice builds up to a roar and quiets down again, over and over:

"It has come to my ATTENTION that this class has REFUSED TO ACCEPT a reading assignment. I have NEVER heard of such blatant DISRESPECT in one of MY TEAM'S classrooms! Why in the WORLD would you think you could get AWAY with something like this?"

He pauses, his red face turning to survey the room. The books are still sitting in their piles at the front of each row. I don't know what the other classes on our team are reading, but apparently it's not the same huge, moldy Charles Dickens classic we are lucky enough to have as our assignment. Mr. Overbye glares at the piles of books as though they are going to jump up and attack him at any moment. Then he glares at every kid in the class in the exact same way, although I am pretty sure he spends a bit of extra time staring me down.

I force myself to hold his gaze until it moves on to Vicky.

"Does anybody have anything they wish to TELL me?" The Bee asks.

Your mustache is a little crooked, I think. *Oh, and you should never wear a pink shirt with that complexion. It makes your face look like a slab of bad salmon.* But even I am smart enough not to share these words of wisdom with the group.

Gradually, I notice all the heads of the kids in front of me are turning toward the back row, where Elizabeth Maersh is raising her hand. Elizabeth Maersh never says anything in class, and she's never been in any kind of trouble. I can't imagine what she's going to say. I hope she isn't about to tattle on Geoff. Or on me.

Mr. Overbye nods at Elizabeth, who says, "Um, sir, the books are very . . . well, they smell . . . uh . . . really bad."

"They SMELL bad?"

Elizabeth flinches, but that doesn't stop her from nodding. Wow, Elizabeth Maersh might be quiet, but she's brave.

Another hand goes up. It's Joanna Ramsey's. She isn't exactly quiet when we are outside school, but in the classroom, she's basically an angel. "It's true," she says. "They smell like, uh, throw-up." Joanna blushes and looks down, but hey—she's brave, too.

"Like THROW-UP?" Mr. Overbye barks. "REALLY?" He glances at Miss Sarisky, who looks like she might start throwing the books at us in another minute. Apparently, this little meeting isn't working out the way she'd planned.

"Oh, come on," she snaps. "Steve, these children are being ridiculous. Just tell them to take the books and stop wasting class time!"

I don't think The Bee likes being ordered around. He looks at her, then at us. Then at her again. I bet he wishes he hadn't even made the long walk down from his office. He is about to open his mouth to say something, but I have no idea what. I cross my fingers under my desk.

Then, behind me, Shanda Hernandez says, "Why don't you smell them?"

Several kids in the class gasp. Miss Sarisky looks like she has just swallowed an entire lemon. Sideways.

"Honestly, Miss Hernandez," The Bee says, "do you really expect me to smell the books?"

"Why not? I mean, if *we* have to," someone mutters from across the room, near the front. I have a feeling it's Jimmy Ryan. I can't believe he and I are on the same side.

"Yeah," Shanda says. "Smell them! They're *nasty*!"

The Bee is trapped. And he knows it. We all hold our breath as he picks up a copy of *Great Expectations* and kind of wafts it toward his face. His head jerks backward.

Yes!

"I, um, I can see what you mean, Miss Hernandez," he says.

Miss Sarisky looks like her head might explode as The Bee continues. "All right, troops. I'm going to ask all of you to just hold on a bit while I explore some options for solving this situation. In the meantime, maybe the class can work on some spelling lists or something."

He backs out of the room. Miss Sarisky's voice sounds like

she has just swallowed a heaping handful of broken glass as she growls, "Class, take out your vocabulary workbooks. *Now!*"

Under my breath, I am humming "We Are the Champions." This may be my new favorite song.

When we get to Miss Sarisky's room the next day, we find a class set of *Great Expectations* in paperback. These copies look almost as old as the hardcovers were, but they don't smell like barf—just plain old dust. And Miss Sarisky is still super irritated with everybody for the entire rest of the week.

It's not a total victory, but I'll take it. We have stood, united, against the I.S. 61 educational machine. And, ever so slightly, the machine has backed down.

When I see Mr. Overbye in the hallway between classes, he puts one huge arm around my collar, pulls me close so nobody else can hear him, and says, "You know you dodged a bullet today, right?"

I nod.

"So you'd better keep your head down for a while. Do you understand me?"

I nod again.

"Good," he says, and gives me a gentle shove toward the hallway that leads to the stage. On my way to band, I keep thinking there's no way I will be able to keep my head down for long. At any minute, the old-lady teacher is going to track Michael and me down, and then it will be all over.

Parents will be called in. There may be suspensions. Or even expulsions!

It figures. The second I get a girlfriend, I'm getting booted out of school. This is rapidly turning into a middle school *Romeo and Juliet*. Or maybe a rock-and-roll *Bonnie and Clyde*. It's probably more like *Bonnie and Clyde*, because Coty and I are outlaws. Wild. Untamed. Ready to laugh at trouble, play crazy beats during scales, lead the drum section in a choreographed dance whenever the band gets to the fast part of the *Rocky* movie theme.

I guess I shouldn't be surprised when our adventures lead to violence. While the rest of the band is getting their mouthpieces and tuning up, we convince Carlton and this super-tall crash cymbal player named Nicholas "Fred" Frederick to help us play the most excellent beat ever. Carlton is pounding away with his mallet on the bass drum, muffling the back head of the drum to make it sound cooler. I am playing the snare drum. Coty is using both hands to play disco-style sixteenth notes on Nicholas Frederick's cymbals while he holds them one on top of the other, like a pair of giant hi-hats. When we are really grooving, Coty tries to get Nicholas to open the cymbals on beats two and four so it sounds like more disco-like. He's a little confused, so Coty starts counting out loud for him: "One-NOW-three-NOW! One-NOW-Fred-NOW!"

We are so deeply involved in this explosion of funk that when Mr. Impolito lifts his baton to silence the band, we completely don't notice. I guess he must try shouting at us, but we're making a lot of noise. So, like the calm and rational man he is, Mr. Impolito takes the massive ring of keys he always keeps on his podium and hurls them at us. They fly right between Coty and me, and smash into Fred's open cymbals.

That gets our attention. In fact, it makes Fred drop both cymbals like they're hot. The effect is pretty dramatic. Coty and I turn our heads to face the podium. Everyone else turns their heads to face us. I don't know what to do, so I bend over and pick up the ring of keys.

"Mr. Impolito," I say, "would you like me to bring these to y—"

"GET! OUT!" Mr. Impolito bellows.

On my way past the podium, I drop the keys in his lap. He doesn't even say thank you.

Mr. Overbye is pretty surprised to see me. "Jordan," he sighs, "do you even know what *keep your head down* means?"

I nod. I am miserable. All I wanted to do was play a cool beat, and now I am facing the firing squad again. Or maybe it's more like a guillotine. A firing squad requires a whole bunch of executioners, but I'm pretty sure the guillotine is a one-man operation.

"So why would you deliberately antagonize your band teacher five minutes after I warned you to keep your head down?"

I crack. It's like Grandma and the bar mitzvah call all over again. My eyes fill up with tears, and I say, "I was nervous. I always drum when I'm nervous."

"And why were you nervous, Jordan?"

"I've been nervous for days," I say. "Ever since Friday. See, there was this lady . . ."

I don't tell him that Michael and I were having a fight. I say we were just fooling around wrestling, and that we're friends. That second part is not completely untrue. But I tell him how she said she was a teacher, took down our numbers, and said we were in big trouble.

Mr. Overbye leans toward me with his chin resting on one hand and says, "Can you describe this teacher for me?"

I tell him about the umbrella and the red hair. Then he bursts out laughing.

"Oh, Jordan," he says. "That wasn't a teacher. She's just some woman who walks by at three o'clock every day. I've been saying hello to her for years. I could never figure out why she always schleps that massive umbrella around. Good thing for you she didn't start swinging it!"

Well, that is very funny. That is just *hilarious*.

I decide that Mr. Overbye has an evil sense of humor.

At lunch, I tell Michael the whole story. He is pretty relieved. He holds out his hand to shake. "Peace?" he says.

"Peace," I say. What a relief! Now I can stop worrying about the whole Jimmy Ryan thing! I am definitely in enough trouble already. "I'm so glad to be done with all this fighting."

"Oh," Jimmy says from across the table, "you're not done fighting."

"What are you talking about?" I ask. "I just shook hands with your cousin."

"Yeah," Jimmy says with a scary chuckle, "but you still have to face—my bodyguard!"

I guess that's Level Three.

18. Attack of the Weird Squiggly Letters

I guess this bar mitzvah thing is really happening, because before I know it, my mom has gotten a family membership at our local synagogue, signed me up for Hebrew school there, and even found a tutor to come two nights a week to teach me more Jewish stuff at home. And it is all hard! I have to learn six thousand years of Jewish history. Plus, I kind of thought there might be less religious stuff to learn for me as a Jewish kid than there is for Christian kids because Jews don't believe in the New Testament of the Bible. I figured if I only had to read the Old Testament, how bad could that be?

Oh, silly two-weeks-ago Jordan! After my first meeting with my tutor, Mr. Levitt, I know how wrong my thinking was. It turns out that, while it's true I don't need to read the New Testament, there's a catch. Jews don't just read the Old Testament; we also have to read several thousand years' worth of rabbis' commentaries on the Old Testament. So, every time I read a story about Joseph or Noah or any of those guys, then I have to listen to Mr. Levitt saying, "This passage is very interesting, because Rabbi Hillel the Elder interpreted it as a comment on the ancient tradition of blah blah blah, while Rabbi Akiva felt it was a reference to blah blah blah." That's enough to make my head swim.

But there's also the Hebrew language to learn. And that's no joke, my friend. First of all, the letters are read from right to left, instead of left to right like the way we read English. Second of all, there are two kinds of letters. There are big squiggly ones for consonant sounds, and little dots, dashes, and other shapes either beneath or next to the big ones to tell you the vowel sounds.

And that isn't even all! Back in the really ancient times, the vowel sounds weren't included, so you had to guess or memorize what the sounds should be. So, if you were trying to write down, "Hi. My name is Bob," in ancient Hebrew, you would just write, "H. M nm s Bb." You can see how that makes things a bit more challenging for the reader.

This matters a lot, because at my bar mitzvah, I will have to read directly from the Torah, which is basically the Old Testament written in ancient Hebrew. So, in the next twenty months, I will have to learn to read the hard stuff.

But wait, there's more! I won't just have to *read* the Torah in front of all my assembled family and friends. Apparently, I will have to learn to *sing* it.

"How will I learn the melodies?" I ask Mr. Levitt.

"You'll memorize them."

Great. So, all I will have to do is read a bunch of consonants in a funny-looking language I don't actually speak, fill in the vowels in my head, and then sing the result from memory. Sounds like a real piece of cake!

One good thing about being an atheist is that you can do it perfectly well in English.

My first day of Hebrew school is pretty miserable, too. All the other kids in the class have been learning this stuff since they were little kids. Meanwhile, I know two consonants and exactly one vowel. Here are the two things I can sound out in Hebrew so far:

1. Bah.
2. Vah.

(My first reading practice session with Mr. Levitt went like this: "Bah. Vah. Vah. Bah. Vah Vah Bah. Vah Bah Bah. Bah Bah Bah Vah." It literally sounded like I was learning how to be an infant.)

This makes me feel like an idiot. All the other kids join in a jolly Hebrew singalong for the first fifteen minutes of the two-hour session while I sit like a bozo looking through the song lyrics for *B*s, *V*s, and "ah" sounds. Even though I get in a lot of trouble in school, I am used to understanding everything we are learning, or at least knowing what the teacher is talking about. Jumping into Hebrew school partway through sixth grade is like getting dropped off in the middle of a class on Mars.

Actually, it's worse, because at least on Mars I wouldn't

know any of the kids, so I wouldn't feel embarrassed about not knowing what was going on. But here at Temple B'Nai Jeshurun, five of my elementary-school classmates are in the room with me. I want to just jump out of my seat and flee, but I keep thinking, *Imagine how proud Grandma will be.*

That is, if I survive until my bar mitzvah. It turns out that Jimmy Ryan's bodyguard is a really tough-looking seventh grader named P.J., who wears a jean jacket with the sleeves ripped off at the shoulders. I guess that's so everybody can see his massive muscles. This dude's arms are thicker than my thighs. He also has a scary stare. His eyes are a faded ice blue, and his hair is such a light blond that you can't see his eyelashes. It's a bizarre effect, kind of like getting stared down by a very pale lizard.

Oh, and P.J. smokes cigarettes! I bet he has hair on his chest, even if the hair is probably so blond nobody can see it. I'm pretty sure he is secretly a grown-up. I'm thinking, *I surrender! Level Two of this game was already too hard for me! Can't I just start over and beat Jimmy up again?*

But of course, surrender is not an option. I can't chicken out now. I try to cheer myself up by telling myself that at least if P.J. kills me, I won't have to keep learning Hebrew. My grandma can just cry a lot at my funeral and wail, "Oh, my poor boy! My only grandson! He never even got to have his bar mitzvah!" And Mrs. Pomerantz and Mrs. Gillary can pat her on the shoulder, hand her tissues, and say, "But, Lillian, the service today was very tasteful. And the buffet is lovely!"

On the day before the fight between my face and P.J.'s knuckles is supposed to happen, an old friend of mine stops me in the hall. His name is Garth, and he is the biggest kid in the seventh grade. You know how in textbooks, when they're trying to show how huge an object is, they put a person next to it to give you a sense of scale? Well, when Garth stands next to me, it looks like a textbook illustration of Mount Everest, with a little tiny dot-sized human beside it for perspective.

Garth and I were on the same Little League team a couple of years ago. I was the tiniest kid on the team and couldn't really hit the ball because of my awful vision. Garth was huge and strong, but incredibly slow, so he wasn't a star, either. We became pals during the dozens of hours we spent side by side on the bench in the dugout. I haven't seen him much since the start of the school year because, aside from band period, the school tries to keep each grade on its own floor. But it's nice to see him now.

"Jordan," he says in his rumbly giant voice, "how's it going? I came to find you because I heard a rumor a seventh grader is going to jump you tomorrow. Do you know anything about that?"

"Yeah," I reply. "His name is P.J., and he's scary."

"And what did you do to him? Why does he want to jump a little bitty guy like you? No offense. I mean, a fine, upstanding Miniature American like you?"

"Ha ha," I mutter. "I didn't do anything to him. I beat up a kid named Jimmy Ryan, and P.J. is Jimmy's bodyguard or something."

Garth raises an eyebrow. "You beat somebody up?"

I nod.

Garth punches me playfully in the arm. "My man! Look at you being all tough."

I smile and try not to rub my arm. "Not tough enough," I say. "What am I going to do?"

"Oh, there's nothing you can do. P.J.'s gonna kill you."

I can feel the smile drain away from my face. Also, I am pretty sure my legs are about to give out and leave me slumping in a heap on the floor.

"Nah, I'm just playing! Leave this to me!" Garth says, whacking me on the other shoulder. I fly into the brick wall of the corridor.

Excellent! I might survive tomorrow's encounter with my new enemy. I mean, if I am not bruised to death by today's encounter with my old friend.

19. Attack of the Killer Seventh Graders

The next morning in band, I am doubly terrified. I can't get my scheduled after-school grudge match out of my head, which is making me nervous enough. But then Mr. Impolito tells us he is going to try something new this year for the spring concert. He's picked out a piece that's so hard, we need to start rehearsing it in the fall, while we are still not done perfecting the pieces for our winter concert. It's called *Festivo*, and for the first minute and a half, it is basically just a really fast drum solo.

Mr. Impolito hands out the sheet music and plays us a recording of the piece. There's one drum part that is too fast for most of the kids in our section to play, but he lines us all up to try out for it. We need three drummers who can all play the super-fast part at the same time: two on snare drums with regular sticks and one on a tom-tom with hard-tipped mallets. The tom-tom part is the hardest, because mallets are really heavy. I figure Coty, Andrew Seligman, and I are all fast enough to start playing this thing. I'm not sure that any of us will be strong enough to keep it up for ninety seconds without slowing down.

Sure enough, the audition comes down to just the three of us. He makes us all try out on the tom-tom. Coty can basically play the part fast enough, but not hard enough. Andrew can play the part fast and hard—for about thirty seconds. Then he starts dragging behind the beat.

"Sonnenblick," Mr. Impolito says, "the part is yours if you want it badly enough. Let's see what you've got."

I play as hard as I can, and manage to keep the pace up for about thirty seconds.

"Metz! Seligman! Snare drums!" Mr. Impolito barks. "As for you, Sonnenblick, you've got the tom-tom. You'd better nail this part. I'm not keeping you around for your sparkling behavior. Or your good looks!"

That went well, I think as we leave the stage. *Hopefully I will still be around for the concert.*

Walking out of school at the end of the day, I can't help noticing that Jimmy and Michael are keeping pace with me. Geoff and Joshua are there, too. Geoff is chattering away, saying things like, "I bet this kid isn't that tough. You just have to use the uppercut! That's all! He's bigger than you, right? So you have to be like, UPPERCUT! UPPERCUT! UPPERCUT! Right in the schnoozer! He'll go down like a tree! Who's the champ? You're the champ!"

I'm doomed, I think.

Garth is nowhere in sight as we get to the edge of the playground fence. On the plus side, neither is P.J. In fact, when we get to the far end of the playground, I still don't see P.J. Maybe if I stay really cool and just keep walking, I can—

Then, all of a sudden, my feet are moving through the air. It takes me a moment to realize what has happened: P.J. has stepped out from behind the fence, grabbed two fistfuls of my jean jacket, and lifted me completely off the ground. Before I can react, he turns ninety degrees and slams my back into the fence of the house that is just past the end of the school's property.

He's pretty quick for a smoker.

"So, you think you're tough picking on a little sixth grader, huh?" he snarls at me.

"Um," I point out, "actually, Jimmy is about four inches taller than I am. Do you think *you're* tough picking on an even littler sixth grader?"

Still holding me up on my tiptoes, P.J. laughs. "I like you," he says. "You're funny!"

"Oh, good," I reply. "Then we can just shake hands and go home, right?"

P.J. turns to Jimmy. "See? Funny kid," he says. Then he lets go of me with his right hand, which he then pulls back and curls into a fist.

I must say, being funny has not turned out to be a very useful skill at I.S. 61 so far.

Just when I think it's all over, a shadow falls across P.J. And me. And basically the whole area. Garth is here! He taps P.J. on the right shoulder. "Hey, P.J.!" he says cheerfully.

"Uh, hey, Garth! What's up?"

"Nothing much. I see you've met my friend Jordan!"

"Your . . . friend?" P.J. asks.

"Oh, yeah. My friend. We go way back. Even our moms hang out."

"That's true," I add. "Our moms are pals. They know each other from Little League. I mean, they didn't play Little League together—Garth and I played Little League together. We were on Lockwood Plumbing. Pretty good team, but we lost to D&L Pizza in the finals."

I don't know why I am still talking. P.J. has let go of my jacket, and he and Garth are only paying attention to each other. Garth smiles at P.J. like we are all just having a great time hanging out, and says, "So how about it, P.J.? Can we all be friends?"

P.J. gives Jimmy a dirty look. I guess facing Garth wasn't part of whatever deal they made. "Sure," P.J. says to Garth. Then he turns to me and grins. "Friends?"

"Sure!" I say. *That sounded too eager*, I think. But I don't care. I am just so happy to be getting out of this alive and with a complete set of teeth.

We shake hands, and then P.J. walks away. Jimmy and Michael follow behind. Joshua and Geoff are still standing with me. Garth says, "Sorry I was late, Jordan. I had math club."

I am still shaking a bit, but I force my voice to sound calm. "That's okay," I say. "I had him just where I wanted him."

"Oh, I didn't come here to protect you. I came to save P.J." Garth throws back his head and laughs. Then he slaps me on the back and walks off.

Wow, I've still got my teeth, I say to myself. Although I think they might be feeling a little loose after that slap.

Geoff and Shoshana approach me at lunch the next day to tell me I have a problem. Coty wants to go out on another date with me. I think about Coty all the time. I am crazy about her! I think this might even be love!

But I am pretty terrified at the idea of doing more kissing. Especially because Geoff and Shoshana (who is now suddenly called "Shosh," which rhymes with "Josh") have done some negotiating, and there appears to be an agreement that on the second date, Coty and I should move on to something called "French kissing." I have to ask what that even is.

Geoff rolls his eyes at me. Shosh says, "You know, it's like regular kissing. But with your mouth open. And, um, tongues."

Tongues? This sounds like a completely horrible idea. First of all, Coty has braces, and I have an appointment to get braces of my own in two weeks. I have heard horror stories about kids trying to kiss with braces on and getting their wires *locked together*. What if Coty and I are on roller skates, and we start kissing, and our braces get all tangled up, and we can't get free? How are we going to transport ourselves from the shadowy kissing platform at the back of Skate Odyssey to someplace where we can get help? We'll have to somehow skate sideways together without being able to even communicate. Then we'll have to find somebody who can call our parents. I can't imagine.

How would the car ride work? Or would an ambulance be involved? Would we wind up in the emergency room, locked together like fighting crabs? Would the doctors have to use some kind of laser to melt through the braces and free us? Would the doctors be able to stop laughing long enough to aim the laser without burning our faces off?

Would the catastrophe end up on the front page of the *Staten Island Advance* the next day? With photos?

The whole thing sounds super risky to me. Also, I just don't think I am ready. But I can't tell them any of this. First of all, anything I say to Shosh will get back to Coty. And second, Geoff has probably been French kissing with fancy private-school girls for *years*. He will tell me I am a *prude*. That is one of the worst things a kid can ever be. It might even be worse than being a *goody-goody* or *afraid of the ball*.

I am just going to have to stall and hope that maybe somehow this will all work out. In a week, I am flying to the Bahamas with my sister and my parents for four days for our first-ever vacation outside the US. So that weekend wouldn't work for a date, anyway. Then the week after that, I will get my braces. Maybe I'll be able to tell everybody my mouth is too sore for kissing for a while after that.

I tell Geoff and Shosh that I am totally interested in a second date, and that I will ask Coty soon.

The first time we play *Festivo* as a whole band, I am very nervous. Mr. Impolito has set up my tom-tom at the very far right of all the other drums, which puts me at the front edge of the stage. I guess this solo is going to be a very visible thing. That's good if I can manage to play it well, but a disaster if I can't.

I wonder which way Mr. Impolito hopes it will turn out. I mean, he wins either way. If I play it perfectly, he's a brilliant band teacher. If I blow it, I'm the idiot with the mallets in my hand. I almost feel like I just lost a game of chess without even knowing I was playing.

Of course, the rehearsal is a disaster. Mr. Impolito keeps stopping the band after we've played only a few measures, and then making just the drum section play. He probably does this five times in a row, which means my wrists are getting super tired from playing so fast with heavy mallets. Of course, that's when he makes me play the solo part all by myself. The whole band is staring. I start off fine but can feel my playing getting slower and slower by the second. I keep thinking, *He'll cut me off now*, but it doesn't happen. He just makes me embarrass myself by playing worse and worse. By the time he actually does cut me off, my wrists are killing me, I am sweating like crazy, and I just want to crawl under the stage and disappear.

"What's the matter, Sonnenblick?" Mr. Impolito asks. I can tell from his tone of voice he thinks this is hilarious.

"Just . . . tired," I pant. "The part is really hard."

"I don't know," he says. "You should be great at this. I mean, *Metz* told me you're pretty fast!"

I can feel my ears burning as the entire band takes a second to get the joke, and then everybody starts laughing. *Don't say anything*, I tell myself with my teeth clenched. *Don't say anything to make this worse.* For once, I listen.

When we move on to the next piece, Coty and I sit down together. I am too humiliated to even look at her, but after a while, she moves her leg so the outsides of our thighs are touching. I look up, and she smiles at me. After a while, she even starts drumming on my leg again. *This is definitely love*, I think. *Even Impolito knows it when he sees it.*

I wish things could stay just like this for a while. Coty and I could just hold hands and maybe play on each other's legs for the rest of sixth grade. Then, in seventh, we could try kissing again. And maybe by the time our braces come off in eighth, I might feel like I know what the heck I am doing.

20. There's Only One Thing Worse Than Getting Saved by Your Sister

I am pretty excited to be going to the Bahamas. I mean, basically, I love anyplace that has lizards, and my parents have told me there are lizards all over the place down there. Plus, our hotel is right next to the ocean. My mom has been going on and on for weeks about the incredibly calm, super-blue, transparent water we will see. We're supposed to go on a glass-bottom boat tour of a coral reef. We might even see sharks! I have been looking at the brochure for weeks, praying I will get to admire a hammerhead up close.

Also, I am bringing Coty's address with me. When I send her a perfect tropical gift, she will know I am the best boyfriend ever. I don't know what the perfect tropical gift is yet, but I am confident I will know it when I see it.

And there are going to be steel drum bands! And foods I've never tasted! (I'm hoping for something with tentacles.) Oh, plus I get to miss two days of school.

But as soon as we actually land in the Bahamian city of Nassau, things start going wrong. First, the hotel hasn't sent a shuttle to pick us up, so we have to wait around in the airport for like a million hours. Then, when we finally get to the hotel, they have given away our room. Lissa and I are both starving, but we can't get any food until this problem is figured out, because until then, we are stuck sitting on our luggage at the front desk.

My parents argue with the front-desk clerk for a while. Then somebody behind the desk has to call the travel agency in New York while my parents argue with each other about whose fault this is. At last, when I feel like I am going to faint right there in the lobby, a manager guy comes out from a back room and gives us some great news: The only room available in the whole place is a "Beachside Villa." Normally, the Beachside Villa costs a thousand dollars a day! But to make up for our "trouble and inconvenience," the hotel will let us stay there for only thirty dollars a day more than what our plain old room was going to cost us.

That sounds like an excellent deal to me. I have never stayed in a Beachside Villa before. In fact, the only place we ever go on vacation is to visit my grandparents in Florida, and both sets of grandparents live more than an hour from the beach. I bet I will see dolphins! Or possibly man-eating sharks!

I mean, from a distance. I am not totally out of my mind.

Unless . . . maybe I will save a tourist from a hammerhead! Then I will be a hero and get on the news. All the kids at home will be jealous because I have become famous *and* missed Miss Sarisky's class—at the same time! When I get back, Mr. Overbye will congratulate me, and even Mr. Impolito will probably say something like, "Okay, Sonnenblick, nice job with the fish thing. Now, hustle over to that tom-tom and get back to work!"

My fantasy is interrupted by raised voices. My dad doesn't want to pay the extra money for the Beachside Villa. He says if we could have afforded to pay more, we would have booked a more expensive room in the first place. My mom is saying, "Come on, Harvey, let's just take the villa. We've been traveling all day, the kids are tired . . ."

The desk clerk and the manager are both apologizing over and over, and at the same time telling us what an incredible bargain we are getting. Dad is furious. Mom is determined to get us out of the lobby and into a room. Meanwhile, Lissa and I are sitting on a mountain of luggage, blocking the path to the desk and looking pathetic.

At this point, they can shove us in a broom closet and I will be happy if it means I can get some food.

Eventually, my dad gives in and agrees to pay the extra money, "at least for now." Soon, Lissa and I are happily munching on potato chips from the hotel's gift shop—"the most expensive potato chips in the world," according to my dad. I think maybe hunger is making him grumpy. We each grab a bag and head out to the back of the hotel. The desk dude said our villa would be easy to find.

The desk dude has never been on a car trip with my parents.

We spend the next half hour dragging our suitcases through a maze of sandy paths, each of which ends at an identical pair of Beachfront Villas. Then it starts pouring. We eventually find our villa, hurry inside, and change out of our soaking-wet clothes. Then Lissa and I go to lie down on the twin beds in our half of the villa. We are supposed to be resting up before dinner, but now that we have had some chips and are done traveling for a while, we are super hyper.

The rain has stopped, so Lissa walks into the other room and asks my parents if we can walk down to the beach and check out the ocean. They agree right away. I am pretty sure they want us out of the way for a while so they can have a really, really big fight without witnesses. As we change at top speed into our swimsuits, I hear my father say, "These people are TAKING ADVANTAGE of us!"

There is nothing my parents hate more than when somebody is TAKING ADVANTAGE of any member of the Sonnenblick family. Once, when I was little, the Wards, who live in the last house at the end of our block, were having a garage sale. I went down there with all of my saved-up allowance money and bought two things: a Daredevil comic book and an opened, half-empty bottle of perfume. I thought my mom would be so, so happy if I surprised her with perfume, especially because the Wards' teenage daughter Lori told me it was a very "sophisticated" gift.

But instead, my mom was unbelievably mad. She grabbed my hand, practically yanked me down the street to the Wards' house, and made Lori give me back my money. She didn't make me return the comic, thank God. But she absolutely slammed that bottle of perfume down on the folding table in front of Lori. It was pretty awkward.

I cried hysterically when we left. I was crushed because my mom hadn't liked my present. "Oh, honey," she said, "it was lovely of you to buy me a present. But that girl was trying to TAKE ADVANTAGE OF YOU!"

This time, my father is the one who is outraged, while my mom appears to be getting outraged at him for *being* outraged. This argument looks like it could get ugly, so I am pretty thrilled to be getting out of the Beachside Villa and hitting the actual beachside beach. Lissa tells me we can't go in the water because we just finished drinking a can of soda each back in the Beachside Villa, and you are supposed to wait half an hour after eating before going in the water.

I would try to argue that drinking is different from eating, but Lissa is strict about this stuff. She is a Junior Lifeguard at the Jewish Community Center. Junior Lifeguards don't play around. So instead of going in, we run up and down the beach for a while, then chase lizards up the trunks of the palm trees that line the paths here. When it feels like we have been doing this for at least seven hours, Lissa says we have digested enough of our soda to make it safe to swim.

But a stiff wind has risen, and there are dark clouds everywhere we look. I can tell Lissa is about to make some new Junior Lifeguard announcement and close down my beach outing, so I whip off my shirt and go charging down into the water before she has a chance. I don't know where my mom got her ideas about the sparkling blue waters, because the waves here are basically sand-colored. Also, they aren't calm. There are huge, crashing waves!

That's okay with me. I like running into huge, crashing waves.

Unfortunately, huge, crashing New York City waves aren't quite the same thing as huge, crashing Bahamian waves. These waves are much huger and crashier. I try diving head-first into one, and it knocks me backward off my feet. I try to stand up, but the wave is carrying me toward the beach too fast. Then the wave comes crashing down, mashing my chest against the bottom, scraping me up, and taking my breath away.

There is a brief, shining half second when the wave has stopped coming in but hasn't yet begun to rush back out. *I am saved!* I think, popping up onto my feet. I manage to take one deep breath before the water starts pulling me backward. I am dragged out fifty feet or so, and then the next wave picks me up and body-slams me again. I can feel the burn of the salt water in the scrapes on my chest, my knees, and my elbows.

The waves throw me onto the sand and suck me back down underwater again and again. It is like I am a very small sock in a very large washing machine. I am starting to think I might actually drown. *Farewell, Coty!* I think as I go under for the seventeenth time. Then I feel a sharp, wrenching pain in the back of my head, and I find myself being dragged up the beach on my back from behind. I blink several times to get the stinging, sandy water out of my eyes, and when my eyes focus, I realize Lissa is pulling me out of the water by my hair.

When I am all the way out of the water, she lets go and I sag back onto the sand, gagging and coughing. "You saved my life," I gasp.

"You are an idiot," she says, wiping her hands against each other to remove the clumps of my hair that cling to them. "You could have *died*!"

That's Lissa for you. She rescues me from sure death, but in the most painful possible way. Then she calls me an idiot.

She cares about me, I think. *She really cares about me!* Then I crawl over to our beach towel, close my eyes, and work on catching my breath.

The whole trip is basically like this. My scrapes hurt. My parents bicker. We cross the island to get to the place where the glass-bottom cruise is supposed to start, only to learn that it has been canceled due to "poor visibility and rough waters."

Oh, the island is suffering from poor visibility and rough waters? That is some extremely useful and timely information. I'm thinking we should have stopped at this pier *before* I took my Swim of Death. My parents take us out for a bunch of fancy meals, and all the restaurants have live steel-drum bands. So at least that should be awesome—but every band plays "The Tide Is High," which makes me miss Coty.

I beg my parents to let me stop in every souvenir shop we

pass, but I just can't seem to find the perfect gift, the gift that screams COTY METZ. She is unique, and all the stupid little polished shells, dorky postcards, and cheesy T-shirts have nothing to do with who she is. Finally, just before we leave for the airport on the last morning, I run into the hotel gift shop and buy her a souvenir spoon ring. This is literally a spoon that has somehow been bent into the shape of a ring. It doesn't look like any of the other tourist stuff I have seen, and it's made of metal so I think it will look nice with Coty's motorcycle-chain belt.

When we are on the plane heading home, Lissa asks to see the spoon ring. As she inspects it, she says, "Wow, Jord. You love her! My baby brother is in lo-o-ove!"

"What are you talking about?" I ask. "It's just a spoon!"

"It's not just a spoon."

"Sure it is! It's a Bahamas spoon! See, it says BAHAMAS right there!"

"Jord, it's a lo-o-ove spoon! Look!" She holds the ring up to my eyes, and I see that there are smaller words before and after the word BAHAMAS. When you twist the whole ring around and read all of it, you get:

SOMEONE IN THE BAHAMAS LOVES ME!

My heart starts pounding. I can't believe this. If I had seen all of the writing, I would have gotten Coty a nice shell instead. I can't give her a big old love spoon and then break up with her over the whole kissing dilemma. *I hate Junior Lifeguards*, I think. *If only Lissa had let me drown, I wouldn't be in this stupid situation.*

The instant we get home, I shove the spoon deep into one of the drawers in my desk. Then I cover it with a pile of old school reports and random stationery, just in case.

A week later, it's time for my big appointment with the orthodontist, which is at six in the morning on a school day. I try to tell myself this will be no big deal. Lots of kids in my class have braces, and Geoff says getting them put on doesn't hurt or anything. He says the orthodontist will just take some pictures and X-rays, and then he will glue a little plastic square on each tooth. The last step will be running one long wire across all my top teeth and a separate one across all my bottom teeth.

"No sweat," Geoff says.

I am thinking Geoff and I must have different orthodontists. The picture part and the X-ray part are just like Geoff said. But then my orthodontist, Dr. DiMarino, says, "Okay, Tiger, I'll be right back to get started!"

Yes, he calls me "Tiger." That should be a warning sign.

An assistant comes in, puts a long paper bib on me, and stuffs my whole mouth with balls and strips of cotton until I can barely breathe. Then she shoves a J-shaped plastic tube under my tongue. When she steps on a switch on the floor, the tube starts sucking all the spit out of the bottom of my mouth.

Seconds later, Dr. DiMarino comes back into the room holding what looks like a black rubber Thor hammer. I want to jump up out of the chair and flee screaming, but I am tilted too far back to make a clean getaway. Also, I think my bib might actually be tied to the back of the chair. Dr. DiMarino pics up a thick, shiny band of metal from a tray that his assistant is holding out.

"We just have to fit one of these around each tooth, Tiger. Not a problem, right?" He punches me on the arm for reassurance. I am not reassured. This metal band is huge! It's practically the size of the ring I bought for Coty. I wonder whether on the inside, it says in microscopically small letters, *Somebody in Staten Island hates me!*

The orthodontist spends the next hour and a half pounding a metal band into place around each of my teeth. An hour and a half feels really long when you are struggling not to suffocate and a madman is hammering away at your mouth. Once in a while, he says something to his assistant, like, "Ooh, that's not going to fit unless we do some bending!" or, "Watch out for that sharp edge, Jamie!" or the worst one, "Oopsie!"

A couple of times when he slips and whacks my lip or my tongue, I can't help making a noise. This is a bad move, because every time it happens, Dr. D. whacks me on the arm again and says, "There's no groaning in baseball, Tiger!"

I have no idea what that even means.

When Dr. DiMarino finally stands up straight and

stretches, I almost tear up with joy. *I am finished!* I think. *I have survived the Mallet of Destruction!*

That is, until he turns to his assistant and says, "All right, Jamie, now we know they fit. Let's take a five-minute break. Then we can come back, pop those babies off, put the cement on 'em, and bang 'em into place again!"

I really have to pee, but I am too busy weeping silently to attempt speech.

My mouth is cut up, swollen, and sore in seventeen different places. On the way out, the receptionist hands me a plastic container of wax and tells me that I can put a little ball of it over any part of my braces that is irritating me. Unfortunately, *every* part of my braces is irritating me. I want to take the rest of the day off to hide out and recover, but my mom takes me straight from the orthodontist to school. Our only stop is to get me a shake at the McDonald's drive-through on Forest Avenue because Dr. D. says my mouth might be a bit too sore for chewing.

Or possibly for the rest of my life, I think. Even sipping and swallowing the shake is an ordeal. But it's not as much of an ordeal as what happens when I get to school. Thanks to the insanely early appointment time, I haven't even missed all of first period. I can't believe I endured all that torment and didn't even get out of seeing Miss Sarisky!

When I walk into class, I work very hard not to open my mouth. I am sure the glittering, twisted mess of metal in my mouth must make me look like the bad guy in a James Bond movie, so my goal is to keep my lips sealed and communicate only by mime for the next two years. Of course, everybody knows I just came from getting my braces, so all over the room, my friends start trying to make me smile. I burrow into my work. We are supposed to be reading silently in *Great Expectations*, which should be a good way to ignore everybody else and keep my dental nightmare private for a while. But a couple of minutes in, I realize I have a new and alarming problem: I am drooling. My mouth is literally filling up with spit, like a really small, really disgusting fountain.

The only way to avoid having the drool run down my chin and onto my shirt is either to choke to death or to make a little sucking sound and swallow the saliva.

Do you know how hard it is to do this in a classroom full of silent readers without anybody noticing? I look up from my book and realize that Vicky Turvey, my seatmate, is looking at me. "Let me see," she mouths.

I shake my head.

"Oh, come *on*, Jordan!" she whispers. "How bad can they be?"

She has no idea. I am somewhat concerned that if I open my mouth too quickly, the concentrated light reflecting off my teeth might actually blind her. I look back down at my book, which lasts until Vicky drops a note on my page:

SMILE!

Again, I shake my head. I try once more to concentrate on the book.

Vicky starts poking me in the ribs with a pencil.

I grit my teeth, which is a painful move, and stare at the page some more.

Just when I think she has given up, Vicky reaches around behind me with one hand so she can poke me in the ribs with both hands at once. I laugh out loud, which means my mouth pops open. Vicky gets the full view of my horrible new mouth.

"Oh, you look *cute*!" she exclaims.

Apparently, the braces *have* blinded her.

21. Attack of the Rubber-Band Warriors

One thing I hadn't realized about braces is how painful they are. Who knew that having two sharp wires and a million little hooks and springs in your mouth would be so uncomfortable? In no time, the insides of my cheeks are all gouged up, and the ends of my bottom wire keep jabbing into my gums right behind my back teeth. Once, the top wire actually impales my cheek. It's in there like a fish hook! Nothing I do will free it, and I don't want to spend the rest of my life speared through the mouth like an unlucky trout, so I have to go back to Dr. DiMarino for some very gory minor surgery.

While I am there, he tightens my braces for the first time. Holy moly! For the next week, it feels like somebody has just punched me in the mouth.

Only one good thing comes from having braces: I get rubber bands! Actually wearing the special tiny rubber bands, which hook on to the backs of my teeth and are supposed to help straighten them, is a terror. They're tight, they make my mouth muscles super tired, and sometimes one of them snaps for no reason, whipping around in my mouth like an angry little rattlesnake. But having a pack or two of rubber bands on me at all times is great fun.

In Miss Sarisky's class, when things get quiet or boring—which is basically all the time—all the kids in the class with braces use our rubber bands to wage a wide-ranging, silent battle. They are a perfect weapon, because they are transparent and so thin that she can't see them flying through the air. As long as she isn't looking right at a kid at the moment of impact, nobody gets busted.

Kids with big, poofy hair are the easiest targets, because they can't feel it when a rubber band lands on their heads. Girls with perms or high hair buns are perfect. So are Carlton with his magnificent Afro; Joshua Stern with his large amount of bushy, wiry Jewish hair (or Jew-fro, as he calls it); and Shoshana, who has a huge, spreading fan of naturally kinky hair. Of course, they are my close friends, so I don't shoot them. I have another target: Ian Goldblum.

Ian is very, very deserving. For a guy who seemed so happy at the beginning of the year, he has been pretty miserable to me. I have gotten perfect scores on two more of those six-problem math things, and now Peter Friedman and I are the only two kids left in the contest from our school. There are maybe thirty-five kids from Staten Island, and something like two hundred in the whole city. I keep meaning to get a problem wrong, but then Mr. Overbye tells me he has bet money on me, or Mrs. Lee stops by my desk and whispers, "Good luck!" and I just can't bring myself to disappoint them.

Well, apparently, I am disappointing Ian. He keeps saying things like, "You think you're so great at math! If you're so smart, why aren't you on the math team?" I want to say, *Because* you're *on the math team*, but I don't. I try to ignore him, but every time I get another six out of six, he piles on the comments: "Just wait till next time! You're going to blow it!" "Good luck! Nobody's rooting for you!" And the dumbest one: "Don't forget to suck up to Mrs. Lee!"

They're math problems, Ian, I think. *Either they're right or*

they're wrong. Sucking up wouldn't help me, even if I did it.
Which I don't. I leave the sucking up to you.

But I don't say a word. As soon as you get drawn into a public argument about how smart you are, you lose. Besides, it's much easier to just wait until Sarisky's class the next day, and then spend the period gently arcing rubber bands onto the top of Ian's pile of frizzed-up hair. If I am shooting at anybody else, I take a fresh, dry rubber band out of the little plastic bag. But when I am shooting at Ian, I get one from my mouth.

The wet ones stick better.

One day, my aim is a bit low, and I hit the back of Ian's neck. He whirls around, snarls at me, and starts feeling through his hair. It's actually pretty funny, because he keeps finding more and more rubber bands. When he has shaken about a dozen onto the cover of a folder he is holding, Miss Sarisky notices that he isn't facing front.

"WHAT is going on over there, Mr. Goldblum?"

"Nothing," Ian says. "I was just . . . brushing my hair. I had an itch."

Wow, I think. *Ian could have told on me, but he didn't.*

Miss Sarisky strides up the aisle until she is looming over Ian. Her nostrils flare, making her look even more like a vengeful ghost than usual. "You had an ITCH?" she bellows. Ian starts to speak again, but she cuts him off. "And what are these . . . things . . . all over your desk? Are these rubber bands?"

Rubber bands are a pretty common school supply. You'd think a teacher would be a bit better at identifying them on sight.

"Yes," Ian says.

"AND WHAT WERE YOU DOING WITH THEM?"

Ian is stuck. Nothing he can say will get him out of this. And it's my fault.

I speak up. "Ian wasn't doing anything with the rubber bands, Miss Sarisky. They're mine."

"Yours?" she asks. "And you expect me to believe they just *flew* here?"

Again, it's like she's never seen a rubber band. "Well—" I start to say.

"I'm holding them for him, Miss Sarisky," Ian says. "He, uh, he's very careless with his orthodontic supplies. He loses them all the time. So yesterday in Hebrew school, I said I would hold a pack for him, just in case. But then the pack broke open in my backpack, and . . . so . . ." This is an amazingly noble lie, but Ian kind of runs out of speed before he gets to the end.

Miss Sarisky just snorts at Ian. Then she strides over until she is standing above me. "Jordan, your teeth have gotten you in quite enough trouble in my classroom. If your conduct in here is not absolutely perfect from now until Christmas, you will regret it *for the rest of your life*. In fact, you would be wise to remain silent in my presence. Do you understand me?"

I grit my teeth and say, "Yes, Miss Sarisky. I will be perfect. I will not lose any teeth or any rubber bands. Just watch. You will be amazed."

"You're absolutely correct, Jordan. I *will* be amazed."

I have to hand it to her. That's a pretty snappy comeback, especially for a lady who doesn't know how rubber bands work.

22. There's Dodgeball . . . and There's *Dodgeball*

Before I.S. 61, I always loved dodgeball. We used to play it at camp all the time. At camp, we played across two side-by-side tennis courts. Each team had to stay on one side of the net on one of the courts, and the area between the two courts, where the benches would be at a fancy tennis place, was no-man's-land. Any ball in no-man's-land could be grabbed by anybody from either team. If you got hit by a ball, you went to jail, which was all the way behind the opposing team. Your teammates could get you back out of jail if they threw a ball completely over the heads of all the opposing players and you caught it on the fly.

Oh, and you weren't allowed to hit anybody above the shoulders with the ball.

At camp, the games were totally fun, and mostly friendly. So in school, when our two gym teachers—tall, thin Mr. Dernback and short, super-muscular Mr. Falcone—announce one day that we are going to be spending a few weeks playing dodgeball, I actually cheer. Then they announce the teams. It's going to be class against class. Also, instead of playing across two nice, wide tennis courts with a no-man's-land in the middle, we are going to play across a basketball court the short way. That means the people chucking the balls are only going to be, at most, twenty-five feet away.

This is a nightmare. My class, 1A, is full of geeky band kids. Our hobbies are things like playing band instruments and learning about computer programming. The kids in the other classes hate us. Their hobbies include threatening us with death in the hallways and stealing our stuff in the locker room.

I don't exactly blame them. Because I.S. 61 is the island's music magnet school, band kids get all kinds of special privileges. How would it feel to watch the band kids getting all the cool field trips, or skipping classes in their red band jackets? Pretty terrible, I bet.

On the other hand, you know what also feels terrible? Getting pegged in the head by a dodgeball that has been launched at missile-like speed by a huge D-class boy and watching him smile, shrug, and say, "Oops! My bad," when the gym teacher blows the whistle. Especially because a *lot* of the boys in the D class are huge. Apparently, kids who don't do band spend their time getting strong. It becomes obvious really fast that this dodgeball unit is going to be a multi-week massacre.

The girls on our team mostly just stand as far back as possible and try to step aside if a ball comes in their direction. So do a couple of the boys. But some of the bigger and more athletic guys in our class are really aggressive. Michael Thompson, Raymond Egan, and James Padilla are our stars. (It is probably not a coincidence that none of these guys are in the band.) Then there are some kids who aren't as big but have great arms, like Joshua Stern.

And then there are Geoff and me. Unfortunately, our strategy is to try to dodge the balls while laughing a lot. After about ten minutes of the first game, it becomes clear that this is a bad game plan, because it makes all the boys on the other team think we are making fun of them. It would be smarter for us to just wear shirts with gigantic targets painted on the front.

Geoff and I don't have great arms. We aren't big or strong. But, thanks to our stunt-related extracurricular activities, we are usually pretty decent at the dodging part of the game. Unfortunately, that just means we end up being among the last players on our team who aren't in jail. And because our arms aren't strong enough to throw the ball all the way over the opposing team to free our classmates without getting really close to the center of the court, when we do get hit, it's usually at extremely close range.

Usually, when 1A plays 1D, it's a relief when we finally lose.

On the last day of the dodgeball unit, we are playing the first of two back-to-back games against 1D, getting killed as usual, when something extra terrible happens. Every kid in our class gets hit except for Ben Bohen, the nicest kid in the world. Who is also the least aggressive kid in the world. Who may also be the nerdiest kid in the world. To give you some idea, Ben carries a briefcase to school every day with a copy of the *New York Times* inside. Ben's eyeglasses are even thicker than mine. He wears a collared shirt to school every day, along with dress pants that he pulls up almost to the bottom of his chest. His hero is Bella Abzug, the noted feminist and former New York congresswoman. Ben has spent every game so far standing way in the back of the class and hoping to get hit by a ball that isn't going a million miles an hour or aimed at his face.

And now Ben is facing the assembled might of Class 1D all by himself. We are all screaming from jail, "Get the ball! Throw it! Get us out of here! WATCH OUT!" Ben gets hit in the chest and the waist by two different balls at the same time, and has to be helped off the court while the kids who hit him are slapping each other five and laughing.

When the second game starts, Ben is on the bleachers behind us, catching his breath. The rest of us are in a rage. Nobody disrespects Ben Bohen like that! Well, I mean, we tease him all the time. But nobody ELSE disrespects Ben Bohen like that! As soon as the whistle blows, we charge up to grab the balls from the center line like we are paratroopers storming the beach during World War II. For a while, we are actually holding our own against 1D!

But then Michael Thompson gets nailed in the stomach.

Raymond Egan tries to reach Michael with a long throw to get him out of jail, but one of the 1D kids makes an incredible leaping catch, and Ray ends up in jail, too. James Padilla gets hit. Joshua throws a ball really hard at the kid who got James, but that kid somehow catches the ball.

Before we even know what's happening, Geoff and I are the only two boys on the court. We try to put up a fight, but it's us against probably ten boys and half of their class's girls. Then Mr. Falcone blows the whistle. "Bohen," he shouts, "get back in there!"

Oh man, I think, *this is not good. This is whatever is the strongest possible opposite of good.*

Ben stands up from the bleachers and kind of tiptoes onto the court. Then the whistle blows again, and suddenly, it's like we are in a shooting gallery. I know there are only five balls on the court, but it feels like about a thousand. No matter how much we twist, dodge, or duck, we can't avoid all the balls. We can't even keep track of all the balls.

Geoff tries to throw a ball to Michael, but his ball gets intercepted. Now it is down to just Ben and me. Well, the good news is that I have always wanted to be a hero. *Here's my chance*, I think as I feel a huge burst of adrenaline rush through me. *I am Evel Knievel! I am Spider-Man!*

"Ben!" I scream. "We have to charge! They'll never expect that!"

"Of course they won't expect that, Jordan—because charging would be stupid!"

That's why it is such an ingenious idea, I think. But Ben hangs back by the bleachers, crossing his arms over his most sensitive areas.

"All right!" I say. "You just stay there and draw their fire. *I'll* charge."

Ben does not object to this new plan. If I am going to charge, I need to be holding a couple of dodgeballs at once. That way, I can throw one to the kids in jail and use the other to block any balls that get thrown at me. I move up halfway to the midline and do a little wiggling dance.

That gets the other team's attention. All five of their team's balls are suddenly flying at me. I dive to the floor, and by some miracle, all the balls fly over me and bounce off the bleachers. I jump up and grab three of them. With one in each hand and one clamped in my left armpit, I am ready to go on the attack!

"Charge!" Geoff shouts from the jail.

Easy for you to say, I think. But I take a deep breath and take three long strides toward the other team, because that's what Evel Knievel would do. Then I hurl one ball as hard as I can on a high arc. I am aiming for Raymond Egan. While that ball is still in midair, I grab the one that had been under my left arm, so now I have a ball in each hand again.

I hear a tremendous thump and a whimper from behind me. Apparently, at least one of the five balls must have rolled all the way back from the bleachers to the other team, because somebody just pegged Ben. Now it is all me!

For about a tenth of a second. I have just enough time to throw a ball at one kid who isn't looking. But of course, I miss him completely. Then I look toward the jail and see that my throw to Raymond has fallen short. The ball is caught by a kid on the other team. I turn to Mr. Dernback, expecting to hear the whistle that will end the game, but he is chatting with Mr. Falcone. The other team is shouting, "He's out! Hey, Dernback, he's out!"

I am about to drop the ball I am still holding, but I don't get the chance. A lightning-fast ball thrown by the other team knocks it out of my hand. This also counts as a knockout, so I have lost twice already. There is still no whistle, but I start to walk sideways off the court.

My third, fourth, and fifth losses all hit me at once, in the knee, the shoulder, and dead center in the middle of my stomach. I crumple to the hardwood, gasping for air and thinking, *What does it take to get a whistle around here?* The whole 1D class cheers as I try not to drool blood on the floor from where my braces have gouged my cheek.

It's easy to be Evel Knievel, I think as the whistle finally blows. *Evel Knievel doesn't have to deal with braces.*

Our next unit is "indoor aerobic exercise," which sounds less scary than dodgeball, I.S. 61–style. Who am I kidding? *Anything* sounds less scary than dodgeball, I.S. 61–style.

Except maybe French kissing. Or the tom-tom solo in *Festivo.*

23. Double Fantasy

One of my favorite activities at camp is minibiking, which is riding small motorcycles on trails through the woods. I am usually pretty good at it, but one day last summer, I had a bad accident. I was going over a jump, lost my balance, and fell sideways. The back wheel of the minibike landed on top of my left side, and the throttle got stuck open so that the wheel was still turning against me until the counselor ran over and turned off the motor.

When he picked me up and asked whether I was okay, I said yes. But on my way down to my cabin after the period ended, I pulled up my shirt and saw that a huge area of skin between the bottom of my ribs and the top of my pants was all chewed up and burned-looking. There was no way I was going to Nurse Klemp with this! She was famous for putting Ben-Gay all over every injury. She would probably slather my gaping wound with half a tube of the stuff. Then I would die of shock.

Fortunately, Peter Friedman was in his cabin next door to mine, so I went over there and asked him for advice. I figured this was a smart move, because first of all, he is a year older than I am, and second of all, his dad is a doctor. Peter took a long, careful look at the big, oozing patch on my side and whistled. "Wow, major motorcycle damage! That's pretty hard-core!" he said.

I couldn't help feeling a burst of pride. If you're going to get a nauseating-looking injury, it might as well be a cool, hard-core one.

"You know you can't go to the nurse with this, right?" he asked.

I nodded.

"Don't worry, though," he said. "I have a whole first-aid kit in my trunk."

Pete pulled the trunk out from under his bed and started fishing around inside. He pulled out a spray can of something called "Sun-Eez," which I was pretty sure was for sunburn. "Okay," Peter said. "All we have to do is spray you up with some of this. It eases pain from minor cuts and burns. Says so right here on the side of the can!"

Looking down at my injury, I felt a horrible sense of dread. I was missing a patch of skin that was about three inches tall and maybe five inches across. That didn't seem minor to me. But my choices were Peter Friedman with his spray or the nurse with a huge blob of Ben-Gay.

I bit my lip, then clenched my teeth. "Go for it," I whispered.

I have had my forehead bashed in by a sharp rock. I have been bitten simultaneously by over a hundred enraged red ants. When I was three, I fell against a brick wall and the corner of a brick ripped open the skin less than an inch from my right eye. I needed stitches to close the gash. None of those things hurt nearly as much as the moment when that sunburn spray hit my skin.

Or really, my lack of skin.

After a minute or so, the insanely fiery burning sensation began to fade and I blinked several times so Pete wouldn't notice the tears that had formed in my eyes. "Thanks," I gasped.

"No problem!" Pete said. "You can come to me anytime!"

Then we headed off to our next activity period. I had swimming. The instant I took off my shirt and the counselor saw my left side, she made her assistant walk me straight to the nurse's office. When I explained to Mrs. Klemp what had happened, she said, "Son, you should have just come straight to me. Don't you know? In the end, *everybody* has to take their medicine." Then she reached for the cabinet where she keeps the Ben-Gay.

I am trying really hard not to have that taking-the-medicine moment with Coty. First there was the Bahamas trip. Then there was the whole thing with getting braces. It's getting more and more difficult to stall, though, especially because we spend all of Miss Sarisky's class gazing across the room at each other, and the whole band period getting in trouble together. And lately, we have been sharing a pack of chocolate chip cookies together at lunch each day, which is kind of painful with braces, but totally worth it. Our school has terrible lunches, but great cookies.

Anyway, it's getting to the point that I look forward to Spanish every day, just so I don't have to be hanging out with Coty, feeling guilty and confused.

Then Joshua Stern's birthday party happens, and I find

myself alone in the basement with Coty, Shosh, Joanna, and Geoff. Somebody has given Joshua the new John Lennon album. We are all pretty excited about it because it's his first album in six years. The other three ex-Beatles have put out something like three albums each since the last John Lennon record. It's nice hearing new music from Paul, George, and Ringo, but John is my idol. For me, listening to new John Lennon songs is practically a religious experience.

Or actually better, because my religion completely baffles me. When I listen to John Lennon, I feel like I am learning the secrets of the universe.

Joshua's basement record player has a pile of albums stacked up—his birthday presents from his family. When the new John Lennon starts, we all just sit and listen for a while. The first song, "(Just Like) Starting Over," is a love song. Somebody kicks me under the table. I look around from face to face, to figure out who is trying to send me a message, but nobody is looking at me except Coty, who is smiling. It's not her usual prankster grin. She is just smiling at me because she likes me.

And I am spending all my time thinking about how we have to break up. I am a jerk.

Suddenly, Geoff and Shosh get up at the same time. "Hey," Geoff says, "we're going to go upstairs and get some cake."

"Yeah. Um, cake," Shosh says, nudging Joanna's shoulder. "Jo-Bo, I bet you want some cake, too. Right?"

I'm thinking, *This is my first time listening to a*

brand-new John Lennon record. Would you guys shut up about the stupid cake?

Joanna says, "Sure, you can grab me a piece. Thanks!"

"No," Shosh says, wiggling her eyebrows like she is trying to communicate some secret message. "You need to *come get your cake.* Right now!"

I can't believe it. They are purposely leaving me alone in the basement with Coty! It's a trap! But for a moment, I think Joanna won't go with them.

Joanna really likes the Beatles.

I guess she also really likes cake. She pushes her chair back, stands up, and says, "Okay, I'm coming." Then she looks back and forth between me and Coty and adds, "Don't have too much fun down here, you two!"

I don't know why it is so freaking impossible to just sit and listen to music around here.

Coty smiles even bigger and slides over into the chair next to mine. I think she must be as into the music as I am, because she doesn't say a word. She just takes my hand under the table.

There are a couple of problems with this situation. One is that we quickly realize something super odd about the album: half of the songs are weird and screechy, because they aren't sung by John. Instead, they are by his wife, Yoko Ono, who sounds kind of squawky, like a very sick crow. The songs alternate, which means every time we get to hear a good song from John, the mood then gets shattered by one of Yoko's, um, unique contributions.

The second problem is that all the songs are about love.

I sincerely hope Coty's hand doesn't drown in the sweat that is pouring off mine. We sit there, nodding through John's songs and trying not to laugh through Yoko's. I don't want to make too much eye contact with Coty, because eye contact might lead to kissing. And kissing might lead to . . . more *advanced* kissing.

By the fifth or sixth song, I am super aware of Coty's leg pressed against mine. I mean, *super* aware. Like I am Luke Skywalker, and her leg is connected to me by the Force. Wait, that seems kind of dumb. Her leg is already connected to me by—well—by my leg. We're practically glued together. *I might faint*, I think. What if I faint, and Coty starts screaming, and everybody comes running down here? And then somebody asks what happened, and Coty says, "I don't know. I just touched his leg with mine and he keeled over!"

There's no way that will look good for either of us.

I may be panicking. Is this what a panic attack feels like? I can feel my heartbeat in the palm of the hand that is holding Coty's. Can Coty feel it? Does she know I am panicking?

Is she panicking, too?

Just as I start to think I might need my inhaler, Coty calmly reaches into her pocket and pulls out a pack of gum. *Okay*, I think, *she is not panicking*. That's good. No, that's bad! If she isn't panicking, *and* she's breaking out the gum, she must be hoping we will start kissing.

When the seventh song comes on, I have two thoughts right in a row:

1. How many songs can there possibly be on one side of an album?
2. How slow are my friends at eating cake?

I won't be able to stand the silence if this is the last song on the side. I jump to my feet. I have no idea why. I am not sure whether my plan was to ask Coty to dance, to put my arms around her and kiss her, or to flee. But when Coty stands up, too, she turns, lets go of my hand, and puts her arms on my shoulders. And suddenly, my body snaps into action. My hands automatically go around her waist. I don't even know how that happened. It's like I am a robot.

Or maybe Evel Knievel. Spider-Man. John Lennon. Some kind of hero.

But would the hero kiss the girl of his dreams, or would he break up with her?

In the end, everybody has to take their medicine, I think. I start to say "Coty" just as she leans all the way in for the kiss.

Then the lights go out.

24. The Sonnenblick Dossier

"Hey, we're down h—" I start to say. But Coty puts her hand over my mouth.

The lights come on again. "Is somebody down there?" a man's voice says. It's Joshua's father. I am saved!

"We're opening presents now," Joshua's dad says. I can hear him slowly moving down the stairs.

Coty doesn't move her hand, so I can't really respond. Joshua's dad keeps coming down until I hear his feet hit the concrete at the bottom of the steps. He is right behind me! Coty's eyes widen. I twist my head around to look.

Mr. Stern is standing there, taking in the view. He has caught Coty and me locked in an embrace, with her hand over my mouth. But he doesn't mention it. All he says is, "Come on up, kids. You don't want to miss the *fun*!"

I decide that Joshua's dad knows exactly what is going on. I feel myself blush as we head upstairs. As we enter the kitchen, everybody's head turns. Geoff, Shosh, and Joanna are all laughing. My face must be redder than Mr. Overbye's. My cheeks must look like they're made of raw steak.

Joshua's gifts from his friends look a lot like his gifts from his family. He already had a great record collection. Now it will be a legendary one. While Joshua is tearing the wrapping paper off an AC/DC record, Geoff catches my eye and gives me a thumbs-up. Shosh smiles at me and gives a little wave. Clearly, everybody thinks Coty and I weren't just listening to John Lennon.

I am more stuck than ever. I can either stay with the girl I like, look cool to our friends, and never be comfortable again, or break up with the girl I like, look like a jerk, and never be happy again.

That Monday, Mr. Impolito has the band warm up with a march called "The Thunderer." Coty and I don't have parts in that piece, so we are sitting together watching Andrew and Lisa play the snare drums. Coty is casually playing the part on my leg. I can't stand the torture for even a second longer! I take a deep breath and say, "Coty, I can't go out with you anymore!"

I can tell she is shocked, because she stops playing. "What? I thought you liked me." Her head tilts downward so she is looking up at me with sad eyes. Coty's eyes are more expressive than other people's eyes. I love looking at them.

Clearly, I am the dumbest person alive.

"I *do* like you," I say.

"But you're breaking up with me?"

I feel miserable. Hurting Coty is like hurting myself. I nod.

"Why?" Coty asks. I might be totally wrong, but I think her eyes suddenly look kind of wet. I am making her cry. I am a monster.

"I don't know," I say.

"But you're sure?" she asks.

I nod again.

"Okay," she says. "Whatever." She starts playing on my leg again, harder. Every time she plays an accent, she moves her stick sideways a few inches so it whacks the top of my knee-cap. This is my first romantic breakup, so I didn't know what to expect, but so far it is at least as painful as I'd thought it would be.

On the last note of the piece, Coty absolutely slams both sticks down on either side of my knee. "OW!" I exclaim.

I hear a throat-clearing noise. I look up from my leg and find Mr. Impolito staring at me. "Are we disturbing you over there, Sonnenblick?"

"Uh, no," I stammer. "I was just—"

"I know, I know," he says. "You were just flirting with Metz."

"No, sir, I wasn't. We were just . . . figuring out our parts."

The whole band laughs, and Coty kicks her leg out sideways and nails me in the shin. I guess that didn't come out right.

"You know, Sonnenblick," Mr. Impolito says, "I've been thinking I should start compiling a dossier on you. Do you know what a *dossier* is?"

"Do you mean a file containing information about me and my activities?" I ask.

Even while I am saying it, Coty is frantically shaking her head at me. So is Shosh, over in the clarinet section. I know I am giving the wrong answer. I mean, it's the right definition. But it's definitely the wrong answer. The right answer would have been something like, "Uh, duh, no! Can you please tell me what a dossier is?"

Mr. Impolito doesn't even say anything. He just points to the door. I try not to limp on my way out.

When Mr. Overbye asks me why I have been kicked out of class *this time*, I don't mention any of the Coty stuff. I just tell him about the definition incident. He sighs.

"Why, Jordan?" he asks.

I am mad. "What do you mean, why? What did I do wrong? Mr. Impolito asked me if I could define a word, so I defined the word. Isn't this a school? Aren't students supposed to be answering teachers' questions here?"

Mr. Overbye clenches his eyes shut and pinches the bridge of his nose like I am giving him a headache. "Jordan, you are one of the smartest kids in this building."

Somehow, he makes it clear that this is not exactly a compliment.

"But," he continues, "there is a difference between smartness and wisdom. You knew your teacher was angry with you, right?"

I nod.

"And you know Mr. Impolito. He has been your band teacher for a few months already. Does he strike you as the kind of man who likes to be proven wrong?"

"I didn't prove him wrong! I just answered his question. And he kicked me out of band for it. He kicked me out of band for *knowing a vocabulary word*! What's next? I answer a math problem correctly and he shoots me in the head? This is so stupid. I don't even want to go back to band!"

This is kind of true. If I don't go back to band, I won't have to face Coty.

"Jordan," Mr. Overbye says quietly. "Think about this. If you don't go back to band, you will have to go to shop class instead. Would you rather be in woodworking? Or metal shop? Or would you rather be in band with your friends, playing the drums?"

"I don't know! Mr. Impolito hates me!"

"Well, he definitely gets, shall we say, *annoyed* with you. But he doesn't hate you. Actually, he tells me that you're quite talented."

I am shocked. "Mr. Impolito said that?"

"Yes. He did."

I am not sure I believe Mr. Overbye. "You're serious?"

He nods.

"Wow," I say. "I guess now you're going to tell me Miss Sarisky doesn't hate me, either."

"No," Mr. Overbye says with a smile, "I'm pretty sure Miss Sarisky hates you. Now, shall I sign you up for shop class, or do you want me to walk you back to the stage to make your peace with Mr. Impolito?"

This time, Mr. Overbye doesn't just make me apologize to Mr. Impolito for being "precocious." He actually makes me and Mr. Impolito *shake hands*, right at the podium in front of everybody. Mr. Impolito doesn't make eye contact with me the whole time and scowls as though accepting my apology has been a physically painful experience. But he does pump my hand up and down three times.

Rather forcefully, in fact.

As soon as I am back behind the drums, Mr. Impolito says, "That's enough marches for today. Let's take out *Festivo*. We'll be taking it just a tad faster today." I scramble to grab the mallets and get to the tom-tom as he begins counting the piece off—really, really fast. Just before the downbeat, he looks me directly in the eye and grins.

25. Silent Days

Coty barely talks to me for two weeks—the longest two weeks of my life. I wish and wish for some kind of gigantic change that will make things okay again between us. But when the change comes, it ruins everything else.

On December 9, my mom wakes me up by shaking my shoulder. At first, I think this is going to be just like any other Tuesday, but then my mom says something I can't understand. This is because she is weeping. What I think she is saying is this: "John Kennedy died!" I have a moment of severe panic, because I know my mom loved President Kennedy, but I also know he died in 1963—six years before I was born.

"What?" I say, grabbing my glasses from the bookshelf over my bed and trying to sit up.

"They shot John Kennedy!" My mom's face is all red and blotchy. Tears are falling from her eyes onto my shoulder as she clutches me tightly to her.

I have no idea what to do. Is there a standard procedure that one is supposed to follow when one's parent is having a breakdown? Probably I should soothe her. I pat her hand. "Mom," I say, trying to make my voice sound as calm as possible, "what are you talking about? John Kennedy died a long time ago."

She grabs my shoulders, pushes me away a bit, and locks eyes with me. "Not John *Kennedy*," she says. "John *Lennon*."

I almost laugh. "John Lennon's not dead. His new album just came out."

"He *is* dead. Oh, Jord, I'm so sorry. It was on the news. Some crazy person shot him last night. The doctors tried to save him, but he died."

I feel like all the air is being squeezed out of my chest. Like I am having the world's worst asthma attack. Everything except my mom's face seems very small and very far away. "That doesn't make any sense," I stammer. "Why would anybody shoot John Lennon?"

"I don't know," she murmurs, stroking my hair.

Something inside me shatters and collapses. I am crying so hard I can't catch a breath. How can John Lennon be dead? I just listened to his record last night. I'm in the middle of reading his second book. I keep thinking it over and over: *How can he be dead when I'm not done with the book?* I even reach out, grab my copy, and open it to see the words inside— as though the ink should have disappeared when the author died.

"You're sure?" I ask.

"I'm sure, bud."

My mother holds me until my eyes are dry. Then she gets me up and walks me through my morning routine. She lays out clothes for me to wear and steps out of my room so I can dress. She leads me to the bathroom, waits outside while I pee, and then comes in to tell me to brush my teeth. She practically feeds me my breakfast—cinnamon toast with sugar. When I see what she is making, I almost break down again. Ever since I was little, cinnamon toast has been my comfort food. It's what she makes when I have a terrible stomach virus and can't digest anything else.

As I nibble at my toast, she places a mug of hot tea in front of me. I almost smile. *John Lennon drinks tea*, I think. But then it hits me: John Lennon *drank* tea. A huge lump forms in my throat, and I can't even think of swallowing anything more.

On the ride to school, my mom turns on the radio, which is tuned to 1010 WINS news radio. As usual, the announcer says, "You're listening to ten-ten WINS—you give us twenty-two minutes, we'll give you the world!" But they don't give me the world. All they give me is every horrible detail of John Lennon's death. Twice.

I feel like somebody has reached down with a giant hand and taken away my world.

Outside the school, the atmosphere is weird. Half the kids are laughing and messing around like it's a normal day. On second thought, it's more like three-quarters. The other quarter—my quarter—are walking like zombies, silent and stunned. I see Geoff standing by the flagpole with Joshua Stern. They are both red-eyed and quiet. "Hey," Joshua mumbles, "I guess you probably heard about—"

"Yeah," I say. "My mom told me."

We stand there, kicking at the ground. I have no idea what to say.

Suddenly, Coty and Shosh are there. Coty gives me a bone-crunching hug, and I feel her sobbing against my shoulder. Her hair smells, well, just like Coty. *Coty is hugging me*, I think for a split second. *Everything is all right!* Then I realize how awful that is. John Lennon didn't give his life in order to fix my romantic situation with my ex-girlfriend.

In fact, I am not supposed to have a romantic situation with my ex-girlfriend. I am pretty sure that is what the "ex" part *means*.

Shosh throws her arms around both of us. "I'm so sorry, Jordan," Shosh says.

"Me too," I mumble, trying not to cry in front of half my class.

Jo-Bo walks up to us, looks from each miserable face to the next, and says, "Guys, what's going on?" When we tell her, she puts her hands over her mouth and tears come to her eyes.

My friends are a mess.

Joshua says, "We have to *do* something!"

Geoff says, "What are we supposed to do? It's not like we can save the guy. He's already dead."

In homeroom, Jimmy Ryan turns to me while I am sitting silently between Joshua and James Padilla. For a second, I think he is going to say something obnoxious, but he surprises me by saying, "Is this ridiculous or what? I love John Lennon. Who would want to shoot *John Lennon*? I mean, the guy wrote 'Give Peace a Chance.' I don't get it."

I am stunned. I just look at him, thinking, *Jimmy Ryan is sad about John Lennon, too. I have no words.*

Then something clicks in my brain. I have no words. I have no words! That's it! We can all be silent in honor of John Lennon! This will bring us all together! And it will confuse our teachers! It's a total win-win.

Except for the part about my all-time hero being dead.

The classroom phone rings, and our homeroom teacher pulls the cord out into the hallway to talk. The whole class breaks into whispers. "Shh!" I say. "I have an announcement to make!"

I tell everybody I think we should be silent at lunch in honor of John Lennon.

I can see heads nodding around the room.

"Let's be silent all morning!" Coty adds.

Now kids are actually looking around the room, smiling at one another. This is great! We are all coming together as one. It's just like the Beatles said. All you need is love.

There's a pause, and then Michael Thompson says, "Let's be silent all day!"

The whole class seems to love this idea.

"And tomorrow!" Joshua adds.

Lots of people nod enthusiastically.

Then Geoff shouts, "Let's be silent all *week*!"

Some people cheer. But others think about how hard it actually is to be silent. Today is only Tuesday. Four days of silence might not be possible. "Why don't we start with just today, and see how things go?" Shosh asks. She is always the sensible one. I wish I knew how to be the sensible one!

When we line up against the wall outside Miss Sarisky's room, people exchange smiles and glances. We are going to do this! Miss Sarisky waves us into the room and asks Ian Goldblum to hand out a worksheet. As he approaches her desk to pick up the pile of copies, she says, "Good morning, Ian!"

Ian nods at her but doesn't speak.

"Good morning, class!" she says.

It figures, I think. *The one day Miss Sarisky is in a friendly mood . . .*

"I said, GOOD MORNING, CLASS!"

Nobody says a word. Everybody just starts scribbling away at the worksheet. Well, at least she can't blame me for this. She publicly ordered me to be silent until Christmas.

"What's going on with all of you today?" she asks.

I have never seen thirty-four kids concentrate so hard on a worksheet.

"Jordan Sonnenblick," she growls, "is this *your* doing?"

Yes, Miss Sarisky, I think. *You've caught me red-handed in the act of committing silence.* But I keep committing silence and simply shrug at her. Then I get back to underlining nouns and double-underlining pronouns.

"WOULD SOMEBODY PLEASE TELL ME WHAT IS HAPPENING?"

Wow, an angry teacher sounds even scarier in a perfectly silent classroom.

We are all just staring at her when Joanna Ramsey raises her hand.

"Yes, Joanna?" Miss Sarisky says, much more quietly. Teachers love Joanna. Well, everybody loves Joanna.

Joanna stands up, walks to the front of the room, and hands her a note. Miss Sarisky reads it aloud:

Dear Miss Sarisky,
We have taken a vow of silence for the day in honor of John Lennon's death. We are not trying to be disrespectful or anything. We are trying to show respect.
Sincerely,
Joanna Ramsey
and the class

"Is this true?" Miss Sarisky asks the class. I am not sure she entirely understands what "vow of silence" means.

Thirty-four heads bob up and down in perfect unison.

"Fine," she says. "But if this is a trick, I will find out."

Okay, that went pretty well, I think.

"I'm looking at *you*, Jordan Sonnenblick."

It's amazing. I may be the first middle school kid in history to get scolded because his whole class is being too quiet.

Word gets around. Mr. Impolito doesn't say anything to the members of my class all through band. In social studies, Mr. Bretstein makes a kind of game of it: He has us write YES and NO on separate index cards, and then asks us tons of fun questions about the prehistoric people we've been learning about. In math, Mrs. Lee actually commends us on our silent demonstration. She even seems kind of touched by it.

The gym teachers, Mr. Dernback and Mr. Falcone, handle the cafeteria. We have started calling them Green Giant and Sprout, after two characters in a series of frozen-vegetable commercials. They are thrilled whenever anybody is quiet in there. It's even kind of fun passing notes back and forth the whole lunch period, especially because we are getting really good at drawing the gym teachers as Green Giant and Sprout cartoon figures.

We split up for foreign languages, so that is fine. But when we get into science, our last class of the day, Mr. Overbye is standing just inside the doorway chatting with Mr. Gallo.

"Come on in, class," The Bee says. He is smiling and sounds kind of friendly, but I still feel a bit nervous. When we are all seated, he adds, "Is there anything any of you would like to tell me?"

Nobody cracks. I feel so proud of my class!

"So it's true, then, what I've been hearing. You have all taken a vow of silence?"

Everybody nods. "Hallelujah!" Mr. Gallo mutters under his breath.

Mr. Overbye clears his throat. "And this is because of the untimely assassination of John Lennon?"

A part of me is thinking, *Is there such thing as a* timely *assassination?* Fortunately, I have taken a vow of silence.

Mr. Gallo and Mr. Overbye exchange glances. "I respect your devotion," Mr. Overbye says. "All right, here's what we are going to do. You may remain silent for the first half of this period. But during the second half, Mr. Gallo has planned a laboratory experiment which involves heating and pouring water. You are going to have to speak during the experiment, for safety reasons. Is that a reasonable compromise?"

I look around. People are nodding. I guess that's fair.

"Good," The Bee says. "And this is a *one-day* event. Am I being clear?"

More nods.

"So tomorrow, you will go back to talking in all of your classes."

"Not too much talking," Mr. Gallo interjects.

"Right. A normal amount of talking," Mr. Overbye says. "Well, for *some* of you, perhaps a slightly-less-than-normal amount of talking." With this, he looks right at me and *winks.*

Again, amazing. I am not sure whether I am more bothered because all the grown-ups automatically think everything that happens is my fault, or because they happen to be right.

* * *

On Sunday, there is a ten-minute silent vigil for John Lennon in Central Park, just across the street from where he was murdered. I beg and beg my parents to take me, and they eventually give in. They even drag Lissa along. It's a freezing-cold, cloudy, windy day, but I don't care. In fact, if you think about it, this is the perfect weather for the occasion. There is a huge crowd, and everybody is bundled up in winter coats, with hats, gloves, and scarves. Even before two o'clock, the time when the official silent part is supposed to start, people are pretty quiet and serious. It's strange, because Central Park is usually such a noisy place, but it's also kind of right.

During the ten minutes of silence, my parents look kind of grim. They aren't crazy Beatles fans like me. My mom says they were a bit too old when the Beatles first came out, so they like folk music better than rock. But they can see how important this is to me. As for me, I can't help myself. If my parents look grim, I must look absolutely devastated. Tears start to come, and they won't stop running down my face. It's so chilly and windy that the salty tears sting my cheeks. My dad hands me tissues one after the other, until my coat pocket is stuffed with them.

Meanwhile, Lissa looks like she is going to die of boredom, but somehow, she makes it through the ordeal.

When people start talking again, my mom gives me a big hug. My parents start to lead us out of the park. That's when a reporter for WINS radio steps into my path and sticks a microphone in my face. "Son, you look to me like a real serious John Lennon fan. Am I correct?"

I nod. Then I realize that's stupid, because you can't hear a nod on the radio. I clear my choked-up throat and say, "Yes."

"May I ask how old you are?"

"Eleven."

"And can you tell me what your name is and where you live?"

"Um, my name is Jordan. And Staten Island."

"Well, Jordan, can you share with our audience at home how you are feeling on this somber day?"

"Uh, I'm sad."

The reporter looks at me like, *No duh, you're sad.* "Can you elaborate on that a bit for our listeners?"

"I'm . . . very sad."

"And there you have it," the reporter says into the microphone. "One tragic day, one very sad fan."

It is probably the most pathetic interview in radio history, but in my defense, I *am* very sad.

26. There Are Lots of Ways to Crash

Every morning before school, Dougie, Geoff, and I go to the candy store across Castleton Avenue. I usually get a Hostess Fruit Pie and a small bottle of orange juice. Dougie gets gum. Geoff generally loads his pockets up with ridiculous amounts of candy and then spends the day handing it out like he's Willy Wonka. One day in early January, though, a kid in Dougie's class named John Fiore dares Geoff to steal a pack of cigarettes.

I beg Geoff not to do it, but Geoff Straniere never turns down a dare—even if it's a really stupid dare.

I love trouble and danger, but not this kind of trouble and danger. My dad's mother smoked, and she died of lung cancer when I was in second grade. It was horrible. I still sometimes have nightmares about the last time I sat on her hot, fever-y lap while she coughed and coughed. Plus, getting caught in school with cigarettes would mean getting suspended—maybe even *expelled*. Shooting rubber bands onto the top of Ian Goldblum's head never got anybody kicked out or killed!

My stomach hurts all day just from knowing what Geoff has in his pocket.

One Friday night, we all go ice skating at our local outdoor rink, Staten Island War Memorial. Dougie and Geoff are both there, and so is Joshua. Plus, there are a bunch of girls from school.

Now, I used to skate all the time when I was a really little kid. In fact, my parents always say I skated before I could walk. Lissa was in training to be a competitive figure skater from the time I was very little until she quit when I was nine, so I basically grew up at her training rinks. Somewhere there's even a picture of me from when I was three, skating behind the Zamboni between sessions. I was like the rink mascot. But I stopped skating when I was five. My mom stepped out onto the ice to talk with Lissa's coach and slipped on a cigarette someone had thrown down on the ice. She broke her leg and had to be in bed for two months!

Mom never put on skates again, and for the next five years, I spent three hours a day sitting down in the snack bar or listening to World War II stories from Louie the skate-rental guy. But this winter it has suddenly become cool to go skating on Friday nights. What am I supposed to do, stay home and miss all the action just because my mother slipped one time, six years ago?

According to my mom, that is exactly what I am supposed to do.

"Jord," she says, "I know you. And I know your friends.

You're going to come up with some kind of stunt and get hurt. I don't want you to spend the next two months in bed while I have to wait on you hand and foot!"

Actually, I think, *that doesn't sound like such a bad deal.*

"Harvey," she says to my dad, "what do you think?"

Normally, my dad doesn't stop me from doing anything just because it might be dangerous. He's the guy who, when I was worried I might get into a fight in elementary school, bought two pairs of boxing gloves and then spent a winter training me. On the other hand, before I was born, he and my mom once tumbled off a sled and he broke his leg really badly.

So he has his own history of winter-sport injury.

I hold my breath.

"I think that, developmentally, it is appropriate for an adolescent boy to spend unstructured social time with his friends." Yes! I have no idea what all that psychiatrist stuff means, but I'm pretty sure he's saying I should go skating.

"Promise me you'll be smart," my mom says to me. "And bring an inhaler!"

I say yes. I mean, I will bring an inhaler.

While Dougie, Geoff, and I are bent over, getting our skates on, Geoff's pocket sort of spreads open and I see the pack of cigarettes. I can't believe he's brought them here! It's not like the skate guards are just going to let an eleven-year-old whip out a cigarette and light up on the ice. I don't say anything, but I get that sick feeling in my stomach again.

On the ice, though, we have a great time. I am a little bit

worried when we first get on that I will be totally terrible, but it turns out that you can't forget how to skate. We start racing around the ice, playing keep-away with people's hats, bumping the girls and shouting "TAG!" and generally being, well, us. Between all that fun and taking breaks to get off the ice and drink hot chocolate, we have enough to do for a great evening out.

But during an ice-resurfacing break, we notice that the Zamboni pushes all the shavings from the rink onto a huge pile just beyond the wooden half wall in the far corner of the rink. This gives Geoff an idea. As soon as we are allowed back on the ice, he leads us over to the corner. We peek over the wall and see that the Zamboni has left a waist-deep pile of snow there.

"Watch this!" he shouts.

Those are never good words to hear coming out of Geoff's mouth.

We wait by the wall as Geoff skates around the entire rink, building up speed. Then he crashes into the wall at top speed, folding at the waist, flipping over the wall, and landing on his back on the snow. We rush over to look down and see whether he is alive.

"Awesome!" he says, spitting out a mouthful of snow.

"How did you do that?" Dougie asks.

"It's easy!" Geoff says. "You just have to make sure the first thing to hit the wall is the toe guards of your skates. The plastic protects your foot, and then you just have to kind of roll over the wall with the impact. Who's next?"

We all line up. Crashing into the wall is even more fun than crashing into Geoff's garbage pile. And there's no smell to deal with. In fact, there isn't even any broken glass in sight. My mom should be thrilled with the responsible choices I'm making!

But then we decide to do a simultaneous three-man crash. It's pretty epic. Geoff, Joshua, and I all end up lying side by side on the snow pile. It's the greatest feeling in the world, looking up into the night sky, watching the foggy breath shoot up from our mouths as we laugh.

Until a face appears over the wall. It's an old lady—even older than our moms! "Are you boys all right?" she asks.

"I saw you hit the wall, and thought for sure you'd have some broken bones."

"Uh, thank you," I say. "But we're fine. We landed on this nice, soft snow—see? It's just a stunt!"

The lady's eyes get all squinty and she says, "You children should be ashamed of yourselves, frightening people like that!"

We all apologize and everything, but the lady just says, "Humph!" and skates away. That makes us crack up for another couple of minutes. When we finally pop up to brush the snow off our jeans and flip back onto the rink, two guards are standing right there. They tell us the old lady complained, and that we had better not do that again.

Here's the thing: We don't do it again that whole session. For us, that is a record-breaking example of self-control. The next week, though, Geoff and I can't resist.

Sadly, skate guards have excellent memories.

The next thing we know, we have been kicked out of the rink. While I am taking my turn at the pay phone outside to call my parents, I hear a *Pfff!* noise from behind me. Geoff has struck a match and lit a cigarette. When I hang up, I beg Geoff to put out the cigarette. My house is only about two minutes away from the rink, and if my mom catches me being a smoker's accomplice, my skating days will be over, maybe even for the whole season!

Geoff responds by holding the cigarette out to me and saying I should take a puff. "Come on," he says, "you'll get a head rush!"

I don't want a head rush. It's bad enough I am now a fugitive from skate-guard justice. I don't need to be an addict, too.

Before Geoff can even finish the cigarette, I see my mom's Chevy Citation in the distance. "She's here!" I hiss. Geoff responds by running and hiding behind a bush.

My mom pulls up to the curb and motions for me to get in. She does a U-turn, rolls her window down, and says, "Hi, Geoffrey!" to the bush.

"Hello, Mrs. Sonnenblick!" the bush shouts back.

My mom scolds me the whole rest of the night about the getting-kicked-out thing, but fortunately, she doesn't seem to have noticed that my friend, the bush, was smoking a Winston Light. The next morning, I call Geoff to see whether he got in trouble. His mother picks up, and as soon as she hears my voice, she says, "Geoffrey is not available to speak with you" in a chillingly cold voice.

It's like she has been possessed by the spirit of Miss Sarisky.

At the candy store on Monday morning, I ask Geoff what happened. "Jordan," he says, "you probably shouldn't call me for a while. My mom smelled the smoke on me when I got in her car. Then I, uh, got dizzy from the cigarette and threw up all over the dashboard. Now she says you're a bad influence."

I can't believe it. The one time I make a semi-responsible choice, I get blamed for making bad choices anyway.

Even when my mom is half wrong, she's still right.

27. Show Your Work!

Mrs. Lee is always getting on me to show my work on every math sheet. She doesn't care if I get everything right in my head. She says that being able to write all the stuff down "in a neat, logical, organized manner" is very important. I always want to know *why* that's important, especially considering I'm one of only two kids in the school who is still 18-for-18 on the citywide word-problem competition. For that, nobody cares about your notes. They only care about your results.

I hate having to jump through hoops just because some grown-up tells me to. When I was in fourth grade and we learned long division, I couldn't understand the pattern of all the things you had to write down in different columns on the paper in order to show your work. I knew how to get the answer in my head every time, but the paperwork just killed me. My mom got sick of hearing from my teacher, Mrs. Fisher, about how "lazy" I was, so she hired her friend's teenage daughter, Karen Lobat, to tutor me.

At our first meeting, Karen told me she would be coming over twice a week until I learned to do long division perfectly.

Karen is the most perfect, beautiful girl on the planet, and I have had a crush on her for years, so I kind of hoped I'd never learn it. Sadly, it wasn't that difficult once she taught me to turn my paper sideways and use the lines to keep my columns of numbers straight. I still didn't see the point, but I learned fast because I *really* wanted to impress Karen.

I'll never forget something she said to me. I asked why I had to learn this dumb process if I could always just get the answers my way. She laughed and then asked, "Do you like it when your teacher yells at you?"

I said no.

"Well, then," Karen said, "that's why. Sometimes it's just easier to give people what they want."

My problem back then, which is still my problem now, is that if I don't like a teacher, I don't want to give them what they want. I don't care if that makes my life harder. Giving in is worse than whatever happens to me if I don't give in.

So, for Mrs. Lee, who is nice and funny and respectful, I try pretty hard to write down some work and make her happy. But when someone like Miss Sarisky, who is mean and disrespectful, tries to get me to write down everything she says in a marble notebook, there's no way I'm caving.

Mrs. Lee isn't exactly fun, but I want to make her happy because of the way she treats me. My Spanish teacher, Señora Gutilla, smiles a lot, and also turns most of what we learn into some kind of fun song, project, or game, so it's easy to do whatever work she assigns. If somebody makes my life more fun, I want to make *their* life more fun, too. My social studies teacher, Mr. Bretstein, has a different way of making us want to learn, but it works on everybody. I swear, I would dive like Daredevil (my favorite Marvel character) in front of a truck full of radioactive waste for Mr. Bretstein. It's simple: He asks us questions. He even asks us, "Why should you want to learn about this?" or, "Do you think this is worth remembering?" Then he sits on the edge of his desk and really listens to our arguments.

Mr. Bretstein doesn't just want us to learn. He wants us to *care*. So when he teaches us that the skull of our prehistoric ancestor, *Zinjanthropus*, was discovered in Olduvai Gorge in Africa by the famous archaeologist-paleontologist Mary Leakey in 1959, I swear I will remember *Zinjanthropus* forever. "Ah, Zinj!" Mr. Bretstein says happily. "Good old Zinj!" One day, he even brings in a model Zinj skull and passes it around. When we've all gotten to hold it, he asks us, "Now, don't you all feel just a little bit closer to the spirit of your ancestors?"

He's excited about the subject, so we are, too.

On nights and weekends, Mr. Bretstein is a Hebrew school teacher. Unfortunately, he is not *my* Hebrew school teacher. My Hebrew school teacher, Mrs. Klein, is like the anti-Bretstein. I started out pretty excited for this stuff, right? I didn't just want to impress my grandmother—I wanted to learn my heritage, my history, *the sacred language of my ancestors*, as Mr. Bretstein would say.

But things have gone wrong with Mrs. Klein pretty fast. Once I felt pretty decent about the Hebrew letters and their sounds, I asked her, "When are we going to learn what all these words we're reading mean?"

She just looked at me like I had two heads and said, "You don't need to know what they mean for your bar mitzvah."

One day in late March, things kind of explode. I am feeling totally hyper and bored, which is made much worse by the fact that it's the first warm day of the year. Our classroom is on the ground floor of the temple. There's a gigantic window behind the teacher's desk that goes almost from the floor to the ceiling, and she has it all the way open so that a warm breeze fills the room. All I want is to be outside, but instead, I am stuck in this pointless class. We spend half of the two-hour session reading and singing in Hebrew without knowing what any of it means. The other half is a Bible lesson. We read a passage in English about how God asked Abraham to sacrifice his firstborn son to prove his faith. Then Mrs. Klein makes a whole big speech about how lots of people in the Bible have to prove their faith to God. Noah has to build his boat, for example, or God will drown him and his family. Another guy, Job, has to go around being tortured by every catastrophe you can imagine just because God has made a bet with the Devil that Job won't lose faith no matter what happens to him.

Mrs. Klein asks the class what lesson we are supposed to

learn from all this. I turn to the girl next to me and whisper, "To stay out of abusive relationships."

When the girl laughs out loud, Mrs. Klein makes me repeat what I've said. I tell her three times that she really won't appreciate it, but she insists. When I tell her, half the class giggles and the other half looks horrified. Meanwhile, Mrs. Klein turns bright red and starts shouting at me about *Rudeness!* And *Disrespect!* And *Sacrilege!*

All of a sudden, in the middle of her rant, a thought pops into my head: *What would Grandpa Sol do?*

Well, duh. I know exactly what Grandpa Sol would do. I grab my books, shove them into my backpack, stand up, and hurl myself out the window. Mrs. Klein yells after me, but I never look back.

There's a beautiful park right next to the temple, with its own lake. I spend the rest of the class time strolling the lakeside path. I start feeling kind of cold after a few minutes, but there's no way I am going back to the synagogue, and it's not like I can call my mom to pick me up early without telling her what has happened. I run back to the temple's circular driveway just in time to dive into our car before the teacher can come out and talk to my mother.

We get away clean.

I have never felt closer to the spirit of my beloved ancestor, Grandpa Sol. But I can't let him know what I've done, because his wife would probably kill both of us. I decide I can't let anybody in my family know. I resolve that, for the foreseeable future, I will just have to get dropped off at the temple, wait until my mom drives off, and then hide out in the park until pickup time.

It's a foolproof plan, except for the part where I am never going to learn enough Hebrew for my bar mitzvah. Oh, and the part where I am lying to my whole family.

The weather stays unusually nice for weeks. The Green Giant and Sprout decide we should go outside to the blacktop playground every day for gym and play an epic four-way kickball tournament. It's actually pretty fun, but one day, classes 1B and 1C get into a heated shouting match on the way back into the building. I am walking with my friends when I hear the commotion behind me.

I don't remember what happens next, but I wake up and find myself looking down at the ground behind Mr. Dernback. He seems to have thrown me over his shoulder and is now carrying me like a sack of potatoes. He is running. Every time one of his feet hits the ground, everything shakes and spins. Something warm and wet is dripping to the ground from my hair.

Then time skips again and I find myself on a bed in the emergency room of Saint Vincent's Hospital, which is right down the street from my school. Mr. Dernback is gone, but now my mother is next to me. A man in a white coat keeps flashing a bright light in my eyes.

The light is pretty, but it hurts me.

The next thing I know, I am in my bed at home. My mom is trying to feed me soup, but I keep gagging. All I want to do is sleep. My father comes into the room, and his footsteps are too loud. I feel all shaky and spinny again. "What happened?" my dad asks.

I am pretty curious, too.

My mom tells him that I was in gym class and some kid threw a rock at another kid, but missed and hit me. Now I have a concussion. I am going to have to stay home from school for a week!

Coty! I think. *Festivo!*

Then I'm pretty sure I don't think anything else for several days.

When I finally start to do things like sit upright again, I find that my mom has been collecting all the work I've missed. I find I can do the work for all the other subjects, but math is now impossible. Clearly, this is serious. Karen Lobat is called in, which is the first good thing that's happened to me since just before the rock hit my skull.

Karen and I spend an hour at my dining-room table. She is trying to teach me how to do very basic equations with variables. Actually, she is trying to reteach me how to do very basic equations with variables, because I used to be good at this during the good old days of last week. I am staring down at the following problem:

$$3x + 2x =$$

I totally understand the concept. Like, I know what an x means and everything. But I can't add 3x and 2x because every time I think about the three, I forget the two. If I try to concentrate on the two, there goes the three! It's like someone has put oil all over the numbers so they keep slipping out of my grasp.

Great, I think. *Now Karen thinks I am stupid. Also, she is probably right. I have lost my ability to think.*

"It's okay," Karen tells me. "Breathe. Take it slow. What's three plus two?"

I look at the three. I look at the two. I look at the three again. I realize I am squinting. My head hurts, and there are little flashes of color at the corners of my vision. "I don't know," I mutter, shoving the papers away from me.

A couple of days after that, I realize I can think about numbers without my whole brain short-circuiting. In fact, aside from a little bit of dizziness if I move my head too fast, I feel pretty normal. I ask my mom if I can try to play my drums. She calls Dr. Purow, who says I can try, but if the noises start to bother me, I have to stop playing immediately.

I go down to the basement. I can feel myself hyperventilating. What if I can never play again? What if I am terrible, and Mr. Impolito demotes me from the Morning Band? I am already dreading it: I will have to look him right in the eye and hand him back my red blazer. I'll probably cry in front of a whole stage full of kids.

So long, tom-tom solo. So long, Coty.

I close my eyes, try to imagine the Beatles in my head, getting ready to play "Drive My Car." This was one of the first songs I ever learned how to play on a kit, way back in fourth grade. I picture John, Paul, and George standing there with their instruments, waiting for me to count them in. *One! Two! Three! Four!* I shout to my imaginary bandmates.

Then everything seems to lurch sideways and I fall off my stool.

28. Step on It!

Dougie Kaner has always been accident-prone. Once, when we might have been in kindergarten or first grade, I was in my house when I heard a horrible scream. My mom, Lissa, and I ran outside to see what was going on. Several members of the Kaner family were crowded around their station wagon. We crossed the Warheits' lawn to get to Dougie's driveway, and saw that Dougie was in the back seat, whimpering and holding his thigh. Apparently, his mom had accidentally slammed the heavy car door on his leg.

A few years later, Dougie, Geoff, and I were waiting in my driveway for the delivery of a brand-new motocross bicycle my parents had gotten me for my birthday. When the truck arrived, Dougie asked me if he could be the very first person to ride the new bike and I said yes. Dougie jumped on, rode down the street to his house, and tried to pop a wheelie while going up his driveway.

Something went very wrong. Dougie flew over the handlebars, landing on his chin. A bunch of paint scraped off the front of the handlebars. Oh, and Dougie needed three stitches.

Basically, if I were Dougie Kaner, I would seriously consider wearing a suit made of bubble wrap at all times.

I am not around to see Dougie's worst catastrophe, though. I only hear about it when I get back to school: Dougie was walking through the Concourse on his way to gym class when all of a sudden, a huge kid came running out of one of the classrooms for the kids with severe behavior problems and threw him to the ground. Then, before the teachers could do anything, the kid jumped up and down on Dougie's arm several times.

Dougie's arm was broken. He had to be taken away in an ambulance!

Between this, the smoking catastrophe, and my rock-to-the-head incident, Geoff tells me his parents are considering moving him from I.S. 61 back to private school. He says he's been begging them not to do it. So far, they have said he *might* be able to stay—if he gets his grades up and doesn't get in any trouble for the rest of the year.

Geoff's worst class is math. The week after I get back, just as my brain starts working again, Mrs. Lee gives a major test. When she puts the exam papers down on my desk, I have a brief moment of panic, but then I picture Karen Lobat saying *breathe*, and I feel okay again.

Well, I might still feel a bit woozy, but that's mostly just from thinking about Karen.

I have no problem at all with the test. In fact, I am shocked by how easy the problems are. A few days later, though,

Mrs. Lee comes storming into the room, slams the pile of papers down, and says, "I have graded your exams, and I have to say I am embarrassed by how poor your results are. We have only a few days left in the third marking period, and I intend to give you another test on the last day. This is my gift to you. I strongly encourage you to study and take advantage of this opportunity to bring your grades up."

Then she walks up the rows, handing us our papers face-down. When I peek at mine and see the red-circled number on top, I quickly shove it into my bag, terrified that someone will see it. All around me, kids are cursing under their breath, and a couple of kids are even crying. Joshua and Shosh are behind me, complaining about their grades. I can't see Joshua's paper, but Shosh has an eighty-five.

"What did you get, Jordan?" Joshua asks.

"I don't want to say," I mumble.

"Oh, come on! How bad can it be?" Shosh asks. "You're, like, Captain Math Brainiac!"

Woo-hoo. That's a title every sixth-grade boy wants. "I'm not saying," I say, more loudly. "It's private."

The phone on the wall rings, and Mrs. Lee turns her back to the class to talk. Shosh and Joshua both get up and stand over me. Shosh starts to tickle my ribs, and when I try to grab her hands, Joshua snatches my paper out of my bag.

"He got a ninety-nine!" Joshua shouts. Lots of kids give me dirty looks.

Shosh glares at me. "I *hate* you!" she says.

* * *

Doug comes back to school with a huge cast on. It goes all the way from his hand to almost his shoulder. He even has to wear a sling. For a while, all the teachers are extremely serious about watching out for fights. There seems to suddenly be an extra supply of teachers, because they cluster up in groups of two and three on every hallway, and at dismissal time, the sidewalk outside looks like a faculty meeting.

Between the increased supervision and Geoff's behavior warning, this would be a disastrous time to get into a fight.

On the other hand, something even more disastrous is going on. During the week when I was at home, lying in my bed of agony, a saxophone player from class 3A named Chris Ferino asked Coty out. I am sad. I am hurt. I am furious! Shosh tells me that I have no right to be mad. She says if I wanted Coty to be my girlfriend so badly, I shouldn't have broken up with her. I say she is still just mad at me about the math test, and she kicks me in the shin.

Extremely hard.

I start making fun of Chris every chance I get. He throws a saxophone reed at me in the band room. It hits me in the face . . . and it's *damp*. This is not an insult that can be ignored. I don't care if there are fifty teachers outside carrying WANTED posters with my face on them. A spitty reed is not something I can back away from.

As we walk outside on the day of the fight, Geoff is giving me some last-minute coaching. "Jordan, listen to me! This kid is short and scrawny-looking, but he's got long arms. So he's got the reach! You have to get inside. Go for the body! If you don't get in there, he's going to pummel you. Okay?"

I nod, but I'm not listening. I am really nervous about this. First of all, Dr. Purow told me I should be extra careful about my head for a while. "Be extra careful" probably doesn't mean "Get punched a lot." But then I think about Chris and Coty laughing together—the way she used to laugh with me. I think about the hollow *thock* sound of that spitty reed hitting my cheek. I start to get excited about punching Chris.

Because there are so many teachers all along the sidewalk, we go through the playground instead. *Great*, I think. *The last time I was here, I ended up in the emergency room.* As usual, we are in the middle of a big mob of kids. The front of the group stops walking, and the usual circle begins to form around us. As I am handing my glasses to Geoff, he grabs my collar, pulls me close, and says, "Remember! Get in there! Get *inside*!"

That would be a great strategy, if not for the fact that Chris Ferino moves really fast. I barely even have my hands up when I feel my head rock back once, twice, three times. "GET IN THERE!" Geoff shouts. "He's killing you!"

If Geoff thinks this fighting thing is so easy, I wish he would consider trading places with me.

I lower my head and charge at Chris, trying to tackle him by the waist. Again, he is too quick. He twists so that when we hit the ground, I am on my back with him sitting on top of me. This is not the ideal position for teaching Chris a valuable lesson.

It is an excellent position to provide Chris with some free punching practice, though. He is busy whaling me in the face, alternating between his right hand and his left, when a whistle blows. Chris jumps up and runs away. Blurrily, I can see a mass of educators heading in my direction.

I can't believe it. The teachers have saved me from getting an even worse butt-kicking. If they catch me, though, I will be in huge trouble. And Geoff will probably be gone! He grabs my hand and yanks me to my feet. My legs are shaking. We start running for the gate at the far end of the fence. When we hit the sidewalk, Geoff pulls me into the street and hands me my glasses. My mom's car is pulled up by the curb across several lanes of traffic. "Duck down!" Geoff orders. We bend at the waist and rush across the street like we are soldiers running under the blades of a helicopter.

Geoff opens the car door and shoves me in first. Then he dives in behind me. My mom is staring at us. Geoff shouts, "Step on it!"

Before pulling out into traffic, though, my mom locks eyes with me. She points to the curb next to our car, where Chris Ferino is crouched down behind a minivan. "You lost a fight to *that* kid?" she asks. *Well, sure,* I think. *He looks pretty small when he's bent over like that. But he's got the reach.*

I can't believe this. My mom isn't mad at me for fighting. She just seems to be amused by how bad I am at it. She and

Geoff make jokes about my defeat all the way home while I try to concentrate on sticking wax on all the places where my braces have sliced up my cheeks.

It feels like a long ride.

I think back on my boxing career, which doesn't seem to be going well. I would say I won the Ryan matchup by a knock-out. Since then, though, it's been all downhill. The Thompson bout was a draw, but only because of the old lady who broke us up before Mike's superior size and strength could really come into play. I had to be saved from P.J. at the last minute by Garth. And now tiny Chris Ferino has taken me down, hard, right in front of my mom.

I think it is time for me to hang up the gloves.

29. "Meet Me at the Corral?"

I walk into the school with a mouth full of wax, a red mark under my left eye, and a sick feeling in my stomach. Everybody knows I have lost a fight to scrawny Chris Ferino. I imagine they are going to be laughing and pointing fingers all day. On the way down the hall to homeroom, Geoff says, "Hey, I'm sorry you got messed up. I did some analysis after the fight, and I realized what our mistake was."

Our mistake? I already know what my mistake was: getting punched a lot. As it turns out, the getting punched a lot was a poor move, strategically speaking.

I don't respond. When we stop at our lockers, Geoff says, "It's so simple, I can't believe we missed it. Listen. Which hand did Chris lead with?"

"What are you talking about?"

"When the fight started. He hit you with his left, right?"

"What's a left-right?"

Geoff sighs. "He hit you with his left hand. Am I correct?"

"Um, I'm not sure if you noticed, but he hit me with both hands. Many times. Forcefully. What's your point?" I'm starting to get annoyed. As my trainer, Geoff has chosen a bad time to suddenly start noticing details like this.

"He's left-handed. He's a southpaw! Just like in the movie *Rocky*. Right? Rocky is left-handed, so he has the element of surprise against a righty. We just need a new training method to get you ready for that left hand. I figure we'll start with some light running to build up your legs. Then we'll get you a punching bag for your basement. And a jump rope, for quickness. Oh, man, this is going to be a great rematch!"

Now it's my turn to sigh. Sadly, sighing hurts my face in about five places. "No rematch, Geoff. Yesterday wasn't really fun, and I feel like I was lucky we got away." I wave my fingers in the air and add, "Besides, I'm a musician. I have to protect these magic hands!"

"Okay," Geoff says. "We can train you for that, too. Let's say five minutes of paradiddles to start, maybe with some extra-heavy sticks. Then five minutes of single stroke rolls, five minutes of double stroke rolls . . ."

The kid is unstoppable.

In Miss Sarisky's class, I notice Vicky Turvey is looking at me very funny. I feel like she's staring at the red mark on my face.

"Does it hurt very much?" she asks me quietly.

I don't know what to say, so I go with, "What are you talking about?"

She reaches over and gently touches the spot with one finger. "This."

"Not anymore," I say. *Ooh, that was smooth,* I think.

"You live around the corner from the stables, right?" she asks.

"Uh, yeah," I say. "Why?"

"Well, I'm there every Saturday morning for my riding lesson. Would you . . . would you want to meet me at the corral?"

For a second, I can't help glancing back toward Coty's seat, but then I realize I won't be betraying her by spending time with Vicky. It's not my fault she's moved on. Well, I mean, it's totally my fault that she's moved on. But if she can move on, so can I.

"Victoria," I say, "I would *love* to meet you at the corral."

In band, Coty and I both spend some time looking down at our feet. Then, just when I can't stand it anymore, Coty nudges the side of my foot with hers. It's not like one of the savage shin kicks that she and Shosh are so good at. It's surprisingly gentle. Our eyes meet and she asks, "Are you okay?"

I nod.

"I'm glad," she says. We sit there for a moment, and I feel pretty peaceful until she adds, "You shouldn't have started that fight."

I rub my cheek and wince. "*Now* you tell me."

"No, I don't mean because you lost. I mean because it was a stupid fight. What did you think, that you were going to win me back?"

"I don't know."

"Because I'm not a *prize*. You can't *win* me."

I look down at my feet again. I feel like a jerk.

Coty isn't finished, though. "Besides," she says, "you never lost me."

"I didn't?"

"Jordan, you could never lose me. You're . . . you're . . ."

"Perfect?" I ask with a smile.

"No, definitely not that. You're just . . . you're just a big *Jork*."

"What's a big Jork?"

"It's like a cross between a Jordan, a big dork . . . and a best friend."

I guess I can live with that.

The night before I am supposed to meet Vicky at the corral, I don't know what to do with myself. I go to the basement, put on a pair of headphones, and play the drums along with the entire album of John Lennon's greatest hits. It's usually the perfect album for relaxing, because it has just the right mixture of slow songs and fast songs, loud ones and soft ones. But as soon as side two ends, I immediately start worrying about the morning again.

I call Geoff for advice, hoping he will be the one who picks up. I am in luck. I tell him I need his coaching. "I've never been alone with Vicky. What am I supposed to do? What am I supposed to say? What do you even wear to walk around the corner from your house and stand next to a corral?"

Geoff takes a deep breath. "Okay, here's the thing. You need to know what kind of girl Vicky is. She's a horsey girl."

"What is that supposed to mean?"

"Her family has money. She likes fancy things. And she's proud of the whole horse thing."

Geoff is a pretty useless boxing coach, but he sure does know a lot about girls. "So, uh, what do I do?"

"Make sure you get there early so you can watch her ride for a while. Then, when she comes over to you, compliment the horse. This is extremely important. When you compliment the horse, you compliment the rider. Ooh, that's really good—hold on while I write it down!"

"Compliment the horse. Got it. And what do I wear?"

"Hmm. Not sneakers. Never wear sneakers in any situation that involves manure. Do you have riding boots?"

"Seriously, who has riding boots?"

"Vicky, for starters."

"No, Geoffrey, I do not own a pair of riding boots."

"What *do* you have?"

"I have snow boots. They're pretty hot for April, but . . ."

"Yeah, no. What else have you got?"

"I have a pair of work boots. Would that be good enough?"

"It'll have to be. Now, she'll probably be wearing a whole riding outfit. But you just need to look like a guy who knows his way around the stables. Have you spent much time around horses?"

"No, I'm super allergic to them. In fact, there's a chance I might start wheezing in front of Vicky. I don't want to bring my inhaler, though. I'll just do a couple of puffs before I leave the house."

"Good call. You're going to wear . . . let's see . . . your most faded pair of jeans. Rips are a plus. And do you have a flannel shirt?"

"Yeah."

"Perfect. Jeans, work boots, flannel. You're all set."

Good God. I am going to look like one of the ranch hands

from *The Wizard of Oz*. "Should I bring along a piece of hay to stick between my teeth?" I ask sarcastically.

Geoff doesn't answer for a minute, like he is really considering this. Finally, he says, "No, I think that would be overkill. Any other questions?"

I feel my face heat up. "Do you think this might be, uh, a kissing situation?"

"My friend," Geoff says, "*every* situation is a kissing situation."

I feel like an idiot as I head downstairs to breakfast all dressed up for a barn dance. Luckily, my mom is out running errands, my dad is doing morning rounds at the nursing home where he works, and Lissa is still sleeping. I leave a note on the kitchen table saying I'm going for a walk, grab my keys, and am almost out the door before I remember I need to use my inhaler.

I rush back upstairs, suck down two puffs, rush back downstairs, and then realize I probably now have inhaler breath. I'm not 100 percent sure there's such thing as inhaler breath, but it's probably best not to take chances. So I run back up, swish around some mouthwash, and charge down and out the front door before I have a chance to think of anything else that might make me late.

Aftershave! I think as I jog up the hill at the top of my block. I turn around and run back home.

By the time I get to the corral, I am a few minutes late.

Also, I am gasping for air and sweating like I have just escaped a house fire. It serves me right for wearing long pants and a flannel shirt on a warm spring day. *Well*, I think, *there's probably nothing else that can go wrong. Unless I get run over by the horse.*

Vicky is there already, on top of a horse that is jogging in circles around the outer edge of the corral. Or cantering. Galloping. I don't know. It's not walking, and she's bouncing up and down. I sit on the fence and watch for a while. She smiles at me from underneath the brow of the—I don't know what you call it—the horsey helmet she is wearing. It's black, and has a round top and a strap that goes under her chin. She is also wearing a white button-down shirt, some kind of plaid jacket, and tan stretchy pants. Plus, of course, a pair of tall leather boots. The jacket, the hat, and the boots make her look kind of like a pretty blonde Sherlock Holmes.

I feel like I should be smoking a wooden pipe and carrying a magnifying glass.

Eventually, she rides over to the gate next to me, slides off the horse, ties its reins to the fence, and steps out onto the street. I jump down off the fence so we are face-to-face.

Wow, I think. *I am short!* I feel a sense of panic sweeping over me. *What did Geoff tell me to do? I can't remember. Oh yeah.*

"Nice, uh, horse," I say.

"Thank you," she replies.

"What's his name?"

"*Her* name is Miss Trixie."

"Oh. Well, with a name like that, I guess it's a good thing she's a girl."

Good save, I think.

"You're so funny, Jordan!" she says, giggling a bit. Her nose kind of crinkles when she laughs. I've never noticed that before. I realize I have never actually talked with Vicky face-to-face, because we are always sitting next to each other in Miss Sarisky's class. Until today, we have basically just mumbled to each other out of the sides of our mouths.

There's a moment of silence that goes on way too long. Miss Trixie neighs. Even she can't stand the tension.

I force myself to take a half step toward Vicky. She leans in.

Oh, wow! I think. *I guess this* is *a kissing situation.* I lean in, too. The brim of her hat hits the top of my head, keeping our mouths roughly an inch and a half apart. For a second, I wish I could disappear. But then Vicky laughs, unstraps her chin strap, takes off the helmet, and shakes her hair free.

Oh, wow, I think again. Vicky is so close that I can smell her. Her scent is a unique mix of flowers, grass, sweat, and just a teensy whiff of horse. It occurs to me that I am allergic to three of those four items. She leans toward me again. The kiss happens.

We chat for another few minutes. Then I go home and have an asthma attack.

Aside from the breathing emergency, I guess it was sort of a nice first date.

30. I Hate Ancient Greek Mathematicians!

I am absent on Monday because of the asthma flare-up. I swear, women are hazardous to your health. When I get to school on Tuesday, I find out we're having our fourth six-problem test in math. I hate taking tests when I am on all my breathing meds. It's hard to concentrate when I am shaking, and my handwriting, which is never the best, becomes basically unreadable. And that's before you consider the tremendous pressure. Mrs. Lee says that if Peter Friedman and I get all the problems right today, we will probably be among the last thirty kids with perfect scores in the whole city!

When I get to the third problem on the test, I know I am in trouble. There is a triangle built into the inside of a rectangle, and first you have to figure out the lengths of the two sides that meet at a right angle. Then you are supposed to use that information to find out the length of the third side of the triangle.

I have never seen anything like this before.

I skip over the problem and rush through the rest of the

paper. When I go back to it, I still have no clue what to do. I am pretty sure that two of the sides are three and four inches long. But I have no idea how those sides are supposed to give me the third side. I am so desperate that I trace the triangle onto my scrap paper. Then I carefully fold it and rip it out, which would be a lot easier if my hands weren't trembling. Finally, I try to hold each of the sides I know up against the side I don't know.

I keep thinking, *Well, if this side is three inches, then how much longer is the one I don't know?* It looks to be almost twice as long as the three-inch side, and definitely a bit longer than the four-inch one. If I had to guess, I'd say it's maybe five and a half inches.

Mrs. Lee tells us that time is up and we have to put our pencils down. Quickly, I scribble down *5.5 inches* in the box on my answer sheet. When she comes over to collect my paper, though, she looks at my paper and shakes her head slightly.

I hate everything. I have spent more than half a year of my life worrying about this stupid competition. I have been repeatedly threatened with having to join the freaking *math team* because of it! And for what? So they could just throw some random, advanced crap on there that there's no way to solve on my own? The test *cheated*!

I am still super mad on the way to lunch. I run into Peter Friedman on the stairs. "Still in?" he asks me with a friendly grin.

"No," I mutter. "I didn't know how to do that stupid third problem."

"The one with the two trains?"

"No, the one with the triangle. I think the two sides were three and four, but I didn't know what to do to get the missing one."

"Oh, that's the Pythagorean theorem. You know, A squared plus B squared equals C squared?"

I shake my head.

"Bummer. You'll probably learn about it next year," he says. "But really, it's eighth-grade stuff."

I don't know what kind of stupid city gives an eighth-grade problem to all of its sixth graders. How was I supposed to get that thing right—use my sense of smell? Mental telepathy? My special secret Ruler-Vision powers?

I might have to move to New Jersey in protest.

Just as I sit down in the cafeteria, Ian Goldblum comes up behind me and asks, "How'd you do? Is the streak broken?" He is smiling. He is always smiling. Grr.

It's one of those times when I don't know exactly what is happening. Somehow, before I can even think, I find myself standing up. But not just standing up—I am pushing Ian's lunch tray upward from below. It flips up against his chest, and when he lowers it again, there's a huge circle of ketchup on the front of his shirt. He is looking at me like I am a dangerous wild animal.

Maybe I am.

Then a very strong hand grabs my shoulder and spins me around. Sprout is standing about an inch from my nose. "Sonnenblick! Goldblum! What is the meaning of this?" he barks.

Ian looks like he is about to cry. I remember how he tried to get me out of trouble after I spent a whole period shooting rubber bands into his hair.

"It's my fault," I say. "I assaulted Ian with his own hamburger. Don't worry. I know where the office is." I turn and walk out of the lunchroom before anybody can see the tears dripping down my cheeks.

I can't stop crying. The Bee doesn't yell. He doesn't even threaten to punish me. He just keeps telling me over and over that I need to think before I act.

Well, duh. If I knew how to do that, would I be in his office?

I keep grabbing more and more tissues from the box on his desk. At this point, I can barely breathe. "I'm going to have to call your mother," Mr. Overbye says.

That's just perfect. I couldn't put my finger on what was missing from my day, but a call to my mom at work is it! Mr. Overbye tells me to wait in the chair just outside the door of his office until she arrives.

My mom's office is less than a mile away, but it takes forever for her to arrive. When she walks in, her face is all pinched up. If there is anything my mom hates more than being interrupted at work, I would hate to ever do that thing. She already looks like she may strangle me.

The Bee calls us both in and asks me to tell my mom why she is here. It's hard to start talking, but once I start, I can't seem to make myself stop. I tell her I am worried all the time about getting in trouble, but no matter what I do, it happens anyway. I tell her that Miss Sarisky goes out of her way to blame me for everything. I tell her that Geoff's mom thinks I am a bad influence. I tell her about the six-problem tests, and how much pressure I have felt all year to get all the problems right. I even tell her I have been skipping Hebrew school.

That last part just kind of slips out.

When I finally finish, she doesn't look mad. She looks super sad instead, which is a million times worse. She asks me to step out so she can talk to Mr. Overbye alone for a minute.

I try not to listen through the door, but I can't help hearing a few words: "Straniere." "Metz." And, most terrifyingly: "Separation." Are they talking about splitting me up from my friends?

I rejoin my class for social studies. On the board, Mr. Bretstein has written OUR FRIENDS, THE GREEKS in big block letters. I try to pay attention, but I am too worried. What is my mom going to do when I get home? What's going to happen to me now that she knows my secret about Hebrew school? And what did Mr. Overbye mean by "separation"?

I am suddenly jolted back to reality when Mr. Bretstein

says, "And then you have good old Pythagoras. You've all heard of him, right?"

I look around. All the kids are shaking their heads.

"He came up with a math formula we still use today. It's called the Pythagorean theorem. You know, A squared plus B squared equals C squared?"

When he sees that nobody knows what he is talking about, Mr. Bretstein draws a triangle on the board. "Okay," he says, "let's say this side here is three feet long. And this side is four feet long. Three squared is three times three. What does that make?"

"Nine!" several kids shout.

"And four times four is what?"

"Sixteen!"

"So if you add up nine and sixteen, that makes twenty-five, right?"

"Yeah!" *Wow*, I think, *people sure do get excited for math when Bretstein does it.*

"So the length of the last side is the square root of twenty-five. And what's the square root of twenty-five?"

Nobody has a clue.

"I mean, what number can you multiply by itself to get twenty-five?"

"Five!" Ian Goldblum shouts.

I have two very strong wishes at once. First, I wish math came after social studies. Second, I wish I had a mustard packet on me so I could finish decorating Ian Goldblum's shirt.

31. Hebrew School Dropout

For about five days, I am a Hebrew school dropout. My parents are really mad at me—not for quitting Hebrew school, but for hiding it from them. My mom says that if I had been kidnapped and killed while I was "wandering around that park alone, like a moron," nobody would ever have been able to figure out what had happened. My dad says that when a man makes a decision, the manly thing to do is face up to the consequences.

My punishment is that I have to call my grandmother and tell her the bar mitzvah is off. All she says is, "Don't worry about me, Jordan. You have to do what is easiest for you."

If making people feel guilty ever becomes an Olympic sport, I nominate Grandma Lillian for team captain.

Then my grandfather gets on the phone. He tells me, "I don't care about the bar mitzvah, as long as you remember this: At some point in his life, every Jew will have a moment when he must stand up and be counted. When that time comes, you will show the world who you are." My grandfather is very big on saying *Stand up and be counted*. It usually comes right after his other favorite saying: *Never again.* All of my elderly relatives say this all the time, because they lived through the Holocaust. Not all of our relatives made it through.

I tell my grandfather I understand. And I think I *do* understand. I mean, if a bunch of Nazis showed up on my lawn, I would definitely fight them. But I don't see what this has to do with my life as a kid in New York City today.

Then two things happen right in a row, almost like a sign from above. I go on a trip to Six Flags Great Adventure with the Jewish Community Center youth group, and I almost get suspended from school.

I have been super excited for the trip for a long time. I live for roller coasters, and Great Adventure has two awesome ones: Lightnin' Loops and Rolling Thunder. Also, I can't wait to be at an amusement park without any grown-ups to slow me down! When our group arrives at the park, all dressed in our matching Jewish Community Center of Staten Island T-shirts, I grab two of my friends from elementary school and run straight for the coasters.

We do every ride that whips you around, crushes you with the force of gravity, flips you upside down, or does any combination of the three. We also eat huge amounts of funnel cake, washed down with giant-sized Cokes. It's a little-known fact, but the more nauseous you are, the more fun the rides become.

I am having one of the greatest days of my life until just before the end. We are supposed to be back at the vans at five o'clock sharp, but at 4:40, my friends and I are stuck in the line for Rolling Thunder. The other boys want to give up and get back to the parking lot. But we've been waiting in line for an hour already, and I can't stand the thought of wasting all that time without getting one last ride out of it. They both decide to go back, but I stay on the line by myself.

I am starting to get a bit nervous about the time, and also about a group of scary teenagers behind me. They're being really loud, they're smoking cigarettes, and they smell like beer. Also, the loudest one is wearing a Confederate flag shirt and saying rude things about the people walking by. I stare straight ahead. I figure there are just two more rides' worth of people in front of me. If each ride takes three minutes, that means I can be done with the ride in nine minutes. Then I can run across the park at top speed and get to the vans just in time!

A ride finishes, and the line starts to surge forward. That's when a hand falls on my shoulder and yanks me backward. It's the Confederate guy. "Move," he says. His breath smells like an ashtray dipped in alcohol. "I'm taking your spot."

"No, you're not. I was here first." I try not to let my voice shake, but I'm pretty sure I fail. I turn my back on him and start to walk forward.

He grabs me again and shoves me completely out of the line while his friends laugh. "I said move, you ugly little Jew!"

I try to step back into my place, and he pulls the front of my shirt until his face is right up against mine. Then he spits on me. It hits my glasses and drips down.

I close my mouth tight, but I can *taste* the spit.

I don't know what to do. I know I can't beat this guy in a fight, even if he didn't have a whole big group with him. He's practically a grown-up. He has a mustache! My eyes fill up with tears as I turn and walk away.

"That's right, you better run!" he shouts after me. *I'm not even running*, I think.

I stop at a water fountain and scrub my whole face over and over again with the front of my shirt, but the taste won't wash away. Then I run back to the van. A counselor yells at me for being late. He asks me what happened to me and why my shirt is all wet, but I am too ashamed to tell him. I don't even tell my friends. I just stare out the window and blink a lot all the way home. I feel like I am going to throw up, but I force myself to keep it down. I realize this is a pointless gesture, but I refuse to give the guy from the line the satisfaction.

I will never eat funnel cake again.

That night in bed, I think about what my grandfather always says. Did I *stand and be counted*? Should I have yelled at the guy until security came, and hoped that he couldn't kill me before they got there? Should I have run away, and then gotten a security guard? What if the guard didn't believe me? Or worse, what if he did believe me, but *didn't care*?

Am I a coward?

I have been trying harder than ever not to get in trouble at school, because I am really afraid that Geoffrey, Coty, and I are going to be split up if we get busted for anything else. It's bad enough that Geoff's mom won't let me see him outside of school. If we don't even have class together, my life will be ruined.

It doesn't help that Geoff and Coty aren't exactly lying low. I'm pretty sure Geoff is failing math, and Coty gets in huge trouble for cursing at a teacher in the hallway. And don't even get me started on what's happening with Miss Sarisky. There's a new shampoo commercial that makes us crack up, and we've turned it into an inside joke about her. The commercial is for a special oily-hair shampoo that promises to make even the grossest hair sparkling clean. The ad is basically just a bunch of different actors pointing at people with dirty hair and shouting, "You've got the greasies!"

So of course, we have developed a whole routine. Somebody pretends to be Miss Sarisky by waving our imaginary fingernails around in the air and saying snotty things. Then somebody else points at the pretend Miss Sarisky and shouts, "You've got the greasies!"

Totally fun and harmless, right?

At least it seems that way until the real Miss Sarisky gets in Geoff's face and sneers, "Mr. Straniere, you've got a serious attention problem."

I feel it coming in the split second before it happens, but there's nothing I can do to stop it. Geoff points her with both hands like he's shooting her with two pistols, and shouts, "And YOU'VE GOT THE GREASIES!"

I have a feeling our days are numbered.

But as things turn out, I am the one who really loses control, in math class. Mrs. Lee is a couple of minutes late. Shanda Hernandez, who sits right behind me, is arguing with Shosh over the answer to one of the homework problems. They are both pretty annoyed, but Shosh is the one with the right answer. I turn around and try to explain to Shanda why her answer is wrong, and she gets really mad.

She yells at me. I snap, "Shut up!"

She shoves the desks aside so she is standing face-to-face with me. Well, sort of. She is a head taller than I am, so it's more like face-to-scalp. She looks down into my eyes, bumps my chest with her crossed arms, and says, "Make me, you dirty Jew!"

I don't think. I just try to shove her away from me, as hard as I can. My hands smash into her stomach. She steps back and crashes into my desk, almost tumbling over it.

Of course, that's when Mrs. Lee walks in. "Jordan! Hallway! Now!" she growls.

She leads me into the math department office, which is in a little alcove across the hall from our classroom. "Sit here!" she says, and storms out, leaving me all alone. I can't believe it. I hit a girl! I've never hit a girl, aside from Lissa. Which doesn't even count, because Lissa is four years older than I am and incredibly strong.

Of course, Shanda Hernandez makes me look like a tiny little guppy. And she called me a *dirty Jew*. For the second time in a week, I *feel* dirty.

When Mrs. Lee comes back in, she says, "Jordan, Shanda says you hit her in the stomach and almost pushed her over a row of desks. What were you thinking? WE—DO—NOT—HIT—GIRLS!"

"She—" I start to say. But, suddenly, I can taste the spit from Great Adventure in my mouth, and I find myself crying so hard I can't catch my breath. Mrs. Lee has to bring me a drink of water and make me sip slowly from it until I can speak again.

"What did Shanda do, Jordan?"

I look down into my lap. I can't even look her in the eye as I say it. "She called me a *dirty Jew*!"

"Oh, Jordan," Mrs. Lee says. Then she shocks me by putting her arms around me and hugging me for a long time.

I still end up getting yelled at, but so does Shanda. And, most important, Mrs. Lee doesn't send me to the office. I wonder whether maybe she understands.

My dad has a mezuzah necklace that his parents gave him on the day of his bar mitzvah. The mezuzah is a Jewish symbol with our holiest prayer written on a curled-up scroll inside it. You're supposed to put a mezuzah on the frame of the front door of your house to mark it as a Jewish home, but you can also wear a smaller one on a chain to show that you are Jewish wherever you go. Even though his parents were very poor, my father's mezuzah is made of real gold.

That night at dinner, I ask my father for two things. I want to go back to training for my bar mitzvah. And I want to wear his mezuzah from now on.

32. Hot Glass and Tweezers Don't Mix

Geoff's mom is still keeping him away from me, so I decide I need to spend more time with my other friends. I start meeting Joshua and Carlton to play tennis in a park near our school. (Each of them beats me every single time, but hey—at least it's exercise.) Joshua and I also begin spending time at Michael Thompson's house, which is something I never would have predicted in September. We always have a great time there. It turns out that Michael is friendly and exceptionally funny when he is not obligated to punch me. Michael has an excellent comic collection, plus there are cool woods behind his house. For a while, there's a new house being built across the street from his house, and we spend hours climbing the beams of the wooden frame.

It's a pretty sad day when Joshua and I arrive at Mike's and find that the construction crew have finished the walls so we can't get in anymore.

The most shocking thing of all is that I start hanging out with Jimmy Ryan. I know it seems crazy, but at some point, I realize that his sarcastic wit is actually a lot like mine. I walk to his house after school a couple of times. Then, one night, I invite him to sleep over at my house.

We are up in my room, laughing and making the spare bed that pulls out from under mine, when my mother knocks on the door. "Jord," she says, "I hope you aren't planning to have a pillow fight."

I am indignant. "Why can't we have a pillow fight? I always have pillow fights with my friends!"

"Yes," she says, "but now you've gotten bigger, and taller, and stronger. I'm afraid someone could really get hurt."

If I have gotten so much bigger, taller, and stronger, that's news to me. I am still the third-shortest boy in my class. Plus, nobody ever gets hurt in a pillow fight. Well, aside from Craig Easton, and that was my mom's fault.

"Mom," I whine, "I already promised Jimmy we could have an awesome pillow fight. I promise we'll be really careful!"

"Fine," she says, "but don't blame me when somebody gets hurt." Then she walks out, slamming the door behind her.

Roughly eleven seconds later, Jimmy and I take off our shirts, change into pajama bottoms, grab our pillows, and start swinging. He hits me in the face, bending my glasses. "Time out!" I shout. "Eyewear time out!" We both take off our glasses. "Time in!" I yell, whacking him in the ribs.

See? I think. *This is totally safe. We're fighting with pillows—how dangerous can it be?*

But then Jimmy gets in three good shots in a row, at my

ribs, my cheek, and the back of my head. I step back, wind up, and go in for a devastating overhead smash. My pillow hits one of the heavy glass globes of my room's dangling overhead light, pushing it to the side so violently that it shatters the light bulb inside. Hot, sharp glass rains down on my bare back.

I fall to my knees on the bed with my eyes closed. I am afraid to look. "Are you okay, Jimmy?" I ask.

"I'm fine," Jimmy says. "But holy crap, your back is a mess!"

"Can you define 'mess,' please?" I gasp.

He grabs his glasses, leans down to take a closer look, and says, "Hmm. It looks like there are some pieces of glass embedded in your back. Actually, there are a lot of pieces of glass embedded in your back."

"Am I bleeding?" I ask.

"Not much. Mostly, the glass pieces seem to be, uh, burned into you."

Burned into me? That doesn't sound good.

Just then, my mom comes barging in. "What was that noise?" she asks.

Jimmy and I exchange glances. He doesn't say anything, but he bites his lip. It is entirely possible that he is trying not to laugh.

"There was a . . . mishap," I say weakly.

"Jord, is that *glass* on your bed?"

Sometimes, there's really no point in answering.

"Jimmy, are you all right?" she asks. He nods, still smirking slightly.

"How about you, Jordan?"

"Um, some of the glass might be, well . . . I have some glass on my back. *In* my back."

My mom, who is very good in a crisis, leaps into action. She tells us not to move so we don't step on any glass. Then she hands me my eyeglasses. I am surprised to see how thoroughly a single light bulb can cover a bed with wreckage. Next, she gives Jimmy his sneakers, brings over a chair for him to step onto, and tells him to stay put until she can get the glass cleaned up. Finally, she hands me a pair of slippers and says, "Follow me."

She leads me into our downstairs bathroom and makes me sit on the lid of the toilet. I watch as she starts lining up supplies on the counter next to the sink. By the time she is done, she has a roll of gauze, a pair of surgical tweezers "borrowed" from the hospital where my dad works part-time, a package of surgical tape, a tube of antibiotic ointment, a washcloth, some Q-tips, and a big bottle of peroxide.

As she turns to get to work on my back, I think, *I guess it could be worse. At least we don't have any Sun-Eez.*

It's pretty bad anyway. Each shard of glass has been fused to my skin by the heat, so each little injury is both a burn and a cut. It probably takes my mom at least ten minutes to remove every single piece, and the whole time, she keeps up a constant lecture, speaking more loudly every time she tugs on a shard. It sounds like this:

"I TOLD you not to have a PIL-low fight! But you WOULD-n't LIS-ten. You're LUCK-y the glass didn't go IN-to JIM-my's eyes. Or YOURS! SOME-times, your mother knows what she's TALK-ing about. Maybe NEXT time you'll pay at-TEN-tion!"

I just sit there and whimper.

When I get back upstairs, my mom supervises as I fold up the sheets to gather up all the pieces of glass. Then she makes the beds with fresh sheets while I have to vacuum the floor in case some of the glass didn't land on the bed.

Or on my back.

Bending over to vacuum is pretty uncomfortable because every time I move, the bandages shift and pull tight against my wounds. When I finally finish, Jimmy smiles up from his chair and asks, "So, Mrs. Sonnenblick, do you think your son might be able to play a nice game of chess without knocking down the house?"

A week later, I am standing onstage waiting for the curtain to open for our spring band concert. I am super nervous. Also, super uncomfortable. At the winter concert, I hadn't really noticed how hot and scratchy my thick polyester blazer was, but it's much warmer in the auditorium in late spring. My white shirt is sticking to my back. Or rather, my white shirt is sticking to my sopping-wet bandages, and the bandages are sticking to my back. I'm not sure which is worse: the itch-ing or the stinging.

But when the curtain opens, I forget about everything except *Festivo*. I am in some kind of a trance during the whole first half. I know I must have played all my parts, but it almost seems to be happening to someone else. Then it's time: I find myself standing at the front edge of the stage with mallets in my hand. Mr. Impolito looks at the snare drummers and mouths, "Ready, Seligman? Ready, Metz?" Then he glances at me and I read his lips saying, "Showtime, Sonnenblick!" as he raises his baton.

I don't have the time or energy to worry about the notes on the page. I don't even really hear the rest of the band. I am too busy trying to hang on to the mallets with my sweat-soaked hands. Before I know it, the fast part is over. Mr. Impolito turns his head to our section and gives us just the slightest little nod, but my knees almost buckle with relief.

We've done it!

I don't play at all in the next piece, so I go over and sit down next to Coty. She bumps my knee with hers and smiles. I smile back.

There's a tradition after I.S. 61 Morning Band concerts. Everybody gets a ride to Pal Joey's, the pizza restaurant, to celebrate. By the time my parents drop me off, most of the tables are all filled up with seventh and eighth graders. The place is a damp, waving sea of red jackets. I stand there in the doorway, not knowing what to do or where to go.

Then someone whistles at me, and I realize I am standing next to a long table full of all my sixth-grade classmates. Ian

Goldblum is waving me over to the only empty seat, which is right next to him.

A waitress brings over baskets of bread. We order pizzas and pitchers of soda for the whole table. But after the pitchers arrive, we sit there forever without getting our pizza. I am so hot I feel like I've just been microwaved on HIGH, but can't take off my jacket because I know my white shirt will be totally see-through from perspiration. The seventh and eighth graders are already finishing up, paying, and filing out of the restaurant while we are still waiting for our pies.

Someone gets restless and shoots the paper wrapping from a straw across the table. Everybody joins in, and when all the straws have been blown, somebody else starts throwing little bits of bread. Then yet another kid purposely spills a soda.

If our food doesn't come soon, I think, *there's a chance things might get out of hand.*

Our pizzas arrive. So does the manager, who immediately starts shouting. He calls us delinquents. I resent that. Before we know it, our pizzas have been boxed up and we are being kicked out of the restaurant. They won't even let us use the pay phone to call our parents! We have to walk all the way down the block to Carvel, which is the only other open place we know that has a phone.

Well, at least the ice cream I buy is cold.

Of course, nobody wants to tell their parents we've been booted out of Pal Joey's, so we stand around the corner from the restaurant and only run over to our cars one by one as they pull up. Geoff, Coty, and I are the last ones to get picked up. When he sees his parents' car at the light in front of the Carvel, Geoff flings the remains of his soft-serve cone at the picture window of the restaurant, where it sticks, dripping bright streaks of vanilla.

I am relieved when I manage to get away in my car without getting arrested.

The next day in band, Mr. Impolito asks one of the eighth graders to lead the tuning-up and gestures for me to follow him into his office. "So, Sonnenblick," he says. "You had some night last night."

"Um, thank you?" I say. It should be a statement, but comes out sounding like a question.

"I have to admit, I had my doubts. But you nailed that *Festivo* part."

"Thank you." There's an awkward pause, which lasts until I clear my throat and add, "Mr. Impolito, why did you give me that part? You don't even like me."

He exhales slowly. Then he says, "Well, Sonnenblick, you're a pain in my behind. But all the best drummers are."

Wow, that was a genuine compliment! Sort of. I nod and turn to leave the office. Mr. Impolito stops me by clearing his throat. I see that he is now smiling thinly. "Oh, there's one other thing. I got a call this morning from Pal Joey's. Is there a chance you know anything about it?"

"Sure," I say. "It's a pizza place. They have great fried

chicken, believe it or not. In a basket. It comes with a side of baked ziti and—"

"Sonnenblick," he barks. I stop talking. "When you are wearing that jacket, you represent me. Do I make myself clear?"

I open my mouth to protest that I didn't start any of the trouble at the restaurant last night, but stop myself. I might not have started it, but I was as guilty as anybody else. Plus, if I argue that it wasn't my fault, he'll just look for somebody else to blame. Like Coty. Or Geoff.

I nod. I hope this story won't end up in my dossier.

33. The End

A couple of weeks later, it's all over. Geoff gets a written warning about his low grades just before we take our final exams, and that's enough to make his mom pull the plug. He'll be going back to private school next year. When there are only two days left in the term, Coty gets called out of class to see The Bee. When she comes back, her eyes are red. She's getting moved to class 3A for the fall.

At the flagpole after school, all our friends stand around Coty, taking turns hugging her. Shosh and Jo-Bo are both crying. It's a mess. Coty saves me for last. "Uh," I say.

"Shh," she says, and pulls me in for a bone-crushing hug. I can't believe this is really happening. I don't want to let go.

When we finally pull ourselves apart, she says, "Hey, we'll still have band every day."

"That's true," I say.

"I mean, if Vinny Impolito doesn't kick you out for good," she adds.

We stand there for a moment. I don't know what to say, but I am not ready to walk away.

"So," I mumble, "how are things going with Chris?"

"Oh, we broke up," she says. "I think we wanted different things from the relationship."

I can't help smiling.

"What about you and Vicky?" she asks.

"That didn't work out," I say.

"Why not?"

The real reason is that I am still scared of whatever is supposed to happen after the first date. But I say, "Well, I decided it was selfish of me to get tied down by one girl. You know, like it wasn't fair for all my female fans and admirers."

"Admirers?" she asks. "Give me a break! What admirers?"

"What? I could have admirers."

"Like who?"

"I don't know. People. You know, *you* used to be my admirer." I feel myself blushing.

Coty kicks me in the shin, but it's kind of a *sweet* shin kick. "You *wish* you could have an admirer like me. You big Jork!"

Then she hugs me again.

My lowest final exam grade is English. When Miss Sarisky gives back the test papers, I see that I got every single multiple choice question right, but I still only got an eighty-five. Turning to the essay section, I see that she has given me a zero out of fifteen for that part.

I know I get in a lot of trouble in her class, but I also know there's no way I deserved to lose every point on my essay. If there's one thing I am good at, it's writing.

"Excuse me," I say to her after the rest of the class has filed out.

She looks up at me. Her facial expression is less than pleasant. "Yes, Jordan," she says.

"Um, I can't help noticing you gave me a zero on my essay."

"True," she says.

I explode. "How could I have gotten a zero? I wrote three pages!"

"It was off topic."

"No, it wasn't," I say. "We were supposed to name two characters from the books we've read, and then show how they were alike or different." I put the papers on the desk in front of her. "Look! Here's the part where I named the two characters: Pip from *Great Expectations* and Beowulf from, uh, *Beowulf*. And here's a whole page on how they're alike. Here's a whole page on how they're different. And here's a conclusion saying they are both alike *and* different."

"It's weak. It's unpolished."

"We had to write this whole thing in half an hour. How *polished* could it be?"

She grabs the paper back from me and says, "You are not getting any points added, Jordan. Nothing you could have written would have been of any value to me!" She sighs dramatically and runs her terrifying fingernails through her tangled hair. I am pleased to note that she's still got the greasies.

*   *   *

There's this teacher whose classroom is the first thing you see when you come through the front entranceway of the school. His name is Mr. Asner, but we call him Mr. Potato Head, because he looks exactly like the toy. He has a gigantic head, ears that stick out to the sides, glasses with thick brown frames, a ring of bushy hair surrounding a large, shiny bald spot, and a large mustache that looks pasted on. We usually have trouble walking by him in the hall without bursting into giggles.

On the last day of school, when we go back to our homeroom after last period to get our report cards, he is standing in front of our class. Looking down at my report card, I see my seventh-grade class assignment:

1A, Asner

Michael Thompson points at Mr. Potato Head and blurts out, "*THAT'S* OUR HOMEROOM TEACHER?" Several of us start to laugh. Mr. Asner glares at Michael, then around the room at the rest of us.

Looks like seventh grade will be another interesting year.

My mom and I spend the last few days of June getting my stuff together for sleepaway camp. My trunk is almost all packed up and ready to go. On top of all the usual clothing and supplies, I've got books and comics, my drumsticks and pad for practicing, and even some Hebrew pages so I can keep my reading skills up. Oh, and of course, I have three inhalers.

Three inhalers *that I know of.*

There's just one last item sitting on the floor next to the trunk: a bulky new eyeglass case. My mom has bought me the dreaded black prescription water ski goggles, and I am not sure whether I should throw them in.

My mom comes into my room and looks from me to the trunk to the case. "It's your call," she says, and walks back out.

I sit there for the longest time thinking about it. I wonder what Evel Knievel would do. What Spider-Man and John Lennon would do. What my grandfather would do. Then I think about how my mom was right when she warned me before my pillow fight with Jimmy Ryan. And how hard it was to walk after I hit the float last summer.

I reach out, grab the glasses, and shove them way down deep in the trunk.

Fine, I think. *I'll pack them.*

But I can't promise I'm going to wear them.

ABOUT THE AUTHOR

Jordan Sonnenblick is the acclaimed author of many novels, including *Drums, Girls, and Dangerous Pie*; *Notes from the Midnight Driver*; *Falling Over Sideways*; *The Secret Sheriff of Sixth Grade*; and *The Boy Who Failed Show and Tell*. He lives in Pennsylvania with his family and can be found online at jordansonnenblick.com.